9-26-07

Thanks for supporting

Hamilton Rotary's Annual Golf Tournament!

Lorna & Reg Wilson

Hamilton Village Real Estate

Hamiltons of the World
THE STORY OF HAMILTONS ACROSS FIVE CONTINENTS

First Published in 2012 by the Hamilton East Rotary Club, New Zealand

Printed by Print House Ltd, Hamilton, New Zealand
in conjunction with Tara TPS, South Korea.

ISBN 978 0 473 21408 1

Cover Photograph, Waikato River, Hamilton, New Zealand

Photograph by Anthony Baker

Contents

5 INTRODUCTION

6 WHERE IT ALL BEGAN

16 IRELAND

24 THE UNITED STATES

150 CANADA

168 THE CARIBBEAN

178 AUSTRALIA

210 NEW ZEALAND

220 AFRICA

228 OTHER HAMILTONS

236 ACKNOWLEDGEMENTS

Introduction

The inspiration for a book about Hamiltons of the World came about as Hamilton East Rotary Club needed a major fundraiser and I felt there had to be a way of utilising the other Hamilton Rotary Clubs around the world, especially as Hamilton, New Zealand is about to celebrate the 150th anniversary of its formation and current name.

When I first emailed seventeen clubs in ten Hamiltons how little I knew where the journey would take me.

Ultimately I located over one hundred and twenty Hamiltons on five continents and while some are simply listed at the end of each section I have managed, with the help largely of Rotary Clubs around the World, to include around eighty Hamiltons in the main text.

What a story Hamiltons of the World turned out to be!

The story has links with, in no particular order - The Chattanooga Choo Choo; A Dutch canal in Sri Lanka; The origins of the game of Cricket; Western Forts and Ghost Towns in the USA; A Mountain in Antarctica; A group of Korean Islands; The 1860 New Zealand Wars; A Bishop in the Czech Republic and many other interesting tales.

It has been great fun, if at times frustrating putting the book together.

Thanks must go to everyone who has assisted me – these are all noted where appropriate – without them all this would not have been possible.

Thank you for supporting Rotary Charities around the World by purchasing this book – I hope you enjoy the read!

Tim Brooker
Rotary Club of Hamilton East, Hamilton, New Zealand   2012

5

Where It All Began

EARLY HAMILTON HISTORY

The cradle of the Hamilton clan is in Hambledon, Hampshire, England. From there a Norman named Walter Fitz-Gilbert of Hambledon moved north to Leicestershire establishing the manor of Hamilton (a derivative of Hambledon) in the parish of Barkby. One of the family, Sir Gilbert de Hamilton, who, in the reign of King Edward II, had killed one of the family of Thomas Despenser (the favourite of Edward II), fled to Scotland. There he married Isabel, daughter of Thomas Randolfe, Earl of Murray. He is first mentioned in Scotland as a witness to a 1294 charter given to Paisley monastery entitling them to fish for herring in the Clyde.

Later, during the Wars of Independence, Fitz-Gilbert was governor of Bothwell Castle on behalf of the English, but he came across to Robert the Bruce's side and was rewarded with a portion of confiscated Comyn lands. Among his new properties was the Barony and lands of Cadzow, which would in time become the town of Hamilton, Lanarkshire.

The family's power grew due to their continued loyalty to the Scottish Crown. In 1346, whilst fighting for David II of Scotland at the Battle of Neville's Cross, Walter's son, Sir David, was captured together with his King and the two were not released until after the payment of an immense ransom.

In the following century James Hamilton married Princess Mary Stewart, daughter of James III of Scotland, and was created Lord Hamilton. Their son was created Earl of Arran, and his son, the 2nd Earl of Arran, served as Regent during the infancy of Mary Queen of Scots.

For his role in negotiating the marriage of Mary to the Dauphin of France, the 2nd Earl of Arran was made Duke of Chatelherault in the French peerage. When he later opposed Mary's marriage to Lord Darnley he was sent into exile but, on his return he sheltered the Queen, following her escape from Loch Leven Castle.

Bothwell Castle, Photograph by Otter

In 1599 the 4th Earl of Arran, Chancellor of Scotland and Keeper of both Stirling and Edinburgh castles, was made Marquis of Hamilton. His brother had earlier been created Lord Abercorn, and was the founder of the Ulster-based Duke of Abercorn line. In 1643 James, 3rd Marquis of Hamilton, a supporter of Charles I, was created Duke of Hamilton and Premier Peer of Scotland. However, following his capture at the Battle of Preston he was taken to London and beheaded. Two years later his brother, who had inherited the dukedom, was killed at the Battle of Worcester.

The dukedom then passed to Anne, daughter of the 1st Duke, who was married to William Douglas, Earl of Selkirk. It was she who initiated the foundations of Hamilton Palace in Lanarkshire. Their son, the 4th Duke of Hamilton, supported the Jacobite Cause. He proved to be an ineffective defender of the anti-Union cause in Scotland. He was created Duke of Brandon in 1711 and died fighting a duel in London.

In the following century, with the additional building of the hunting lodge known as Chatelherault, Hamilton Palace was extended and filled with spectacular collections of art. The Hamiltons lived in great style and, in 1843, William, 11th Duke of Hamilton

Lennoxlove. Photograph by Kevin Rae

Chatelherault. Photograph by South Lanarkshire D.C

Hamilton Palace

and 8th Duke of Brandon, married Princess Marie of Baden, a cousin of Napoleon III. Their daughter, Lady Mary, married Albert I, Prince of Monaco.

In the early part of the 20th century, Hamilton Palace was found to be sinking, a consequence of the extensive coal mining operations in the area. It was demolished between 1922 and 1932 and the family re-located to Lennoxlove in East Lothian.

The Bat and Ball, Hambledon. Photograph by David Brown

Modern Hambledon Cricket Club Pavilion. Photograph by David Brown

HAMBLEDON

Hambledon is a small village and civil parish in the county of Hampshire in England, situated about 15 miles north of Portsmouth.

Despite being the start of the Hamilton Story, Hambledon is best known as the 'Cradle of Cricket'. It is thought that the Hambledon Club, one of the oldest cricket clubs known, was formed about 1750. Hambledon was England's leading cricket club from about 1765 until the formation of the Marylebone Cricket Club (MCC) in 1787.

The famous Bat and Ball Inn in Hyden Farm Lane, Clanfield is next to the historic cricket ground near Broadhalfpenny Down where the Hambledon Club originally played. The inn was run by Richard Nyren, who was also captain of the club. As a venue for first-class cricket, Broadhalfpenny Down was used from 1753 (the recently discovered earliest definite date) until 1781, after which the Hambledon Club moved to Windmill Down, which is closer to the village.

Subsequently, an England XI v Hambledon fixture in 1908 appears in the generally accepted list of first-class fixtures. This was intended as a commemorative match and featured famous players C. B. Fry and Phil Mead.

Hampshire cricketer Edward Whalley-Tooker, who played in the 1908 match, was a descendant of a member of the original Hambledon Club. Following the match in 1908 the Broadhalfpenny Down ground was reclaimed for farming land. Whalley-Tooker set about the task of securing its use for cricket once again and in 1925 it was restored to host cricket matches. The possession of the land was transferred to Winchester College, with the College and Hambledon playing the first match there since its restoration. Whalley-Tooker led the Hambledon side to victory.

The name of the ground, "Broadhalfpenny" is properly pronounced "broad ha'penny" a contraction following the usual pronunciation of the word for the halfpenny coin.

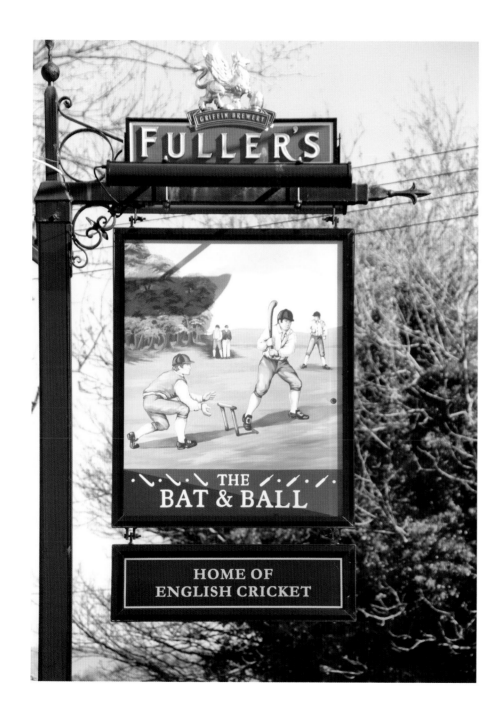

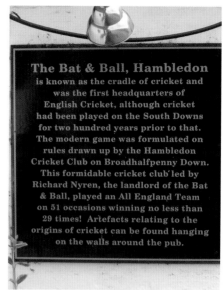

Above: Monument to Hambledon C.C. and Commemorative Plaque.
Photographs by Ben Shade.
Left: Pub Sign. Photograph by David Brown

Places that had obtained a charter from the King to hold markets or establish fairs were issued with Letters Patent that were stamped with "Broad-Halfpenny".

The modern Hambledon Cricket Club's ground is at Ridge Meadow, about half a mile away. Hambledon is now a rural village surrounded by fields and woods. There are about 400 households with just under 1,000 residents.

HAMILTON, SOUTH LANARKSHIRE, SCOTLAND, 1445

Hamilton is about 20 miles to the east of Glasgow in Central Scotland and is part of the South Lanarkshire Council area, having a population of around 50,000.

Hamilton was originally known as Cadzow, derived from the Celtic word Cadihou, the name of the 6th Century summer hunting lodge of Rederech, ruler of the ancient Kingdom of Strathclyde. It was here in 568AD that St Kentigern (St Mungo), the patron saint of Glasgow, converted the King of the Britons and his Queen, Langoreth to Christianity.

During the 12th Century the area was created a Royal Barony by David I of Scotland and under the rule of Robert the Bruce, it was given to Walter Fitz-Gilbert.

During the Wars of Scottish Independence the Hamilton family initially supported the English and Walter Fitz-Gilbert (the head of the Hamilton family) was governor of Bothwell Castle on behalf of the English. However, he later changed loyalty to Robert the Bruce, following the Battle of Bannockburn, and ceded Bothwell to him. For this act, he was rewarded with a portion of land which had been forfeited by the Comyns at Dalserf and later the Barony and lands of Cadzow, which in time would become the town of Hamilton.

Walter's descendant Sir James Hamilton married Mary Stewart, the daughter of King James II of Scotland, and was created Lord Hamilton. The Barony continued to be called Cadzow until 1445 when a charter from James II of Scotland to the first Lord Hamilton allowed the town and district to be renamed Hamilton. It became a Royal Burgh in 1548-49.

The Hamilton family have been major land-owners in the area to this day. Hamilton Palace was the historic seat of the Dukes of Hamilton until the early twentieth century.

Hamilton Palace was the largest non-royal residence in the Western world, located in the north-east of the town. A former seat of the Dukes of Hamilton, it was built in 1695. It was subsequently much enlarged, and demolished in 1921 due to ground

Above Right: Hamilton Old Parish Church. Photograph by Supergolden
Below Right: Hamilton Town Hall

Above: Hamilton Mausoleum. Photograph by G.Laird
Left: Hamilton Racecourse

subsidence. It is widely acknowledged as having been one of the grandest houses in Scotland, was visited and admired by Queen Victoria, and was written about by Daniel Defoe.

Cadzow Castle, originally built during the reign of Alexander II of Scotland on the site of the hunting lodge, was rebuilt around 1530 for Sir James Hamilton of Finnart who, in 1568, gave shelter to Mary, Queen of Scots, after her dramatic escape from Loch Leven Castle. The town and castle were subsequently razed by the Crown in reprisal against the actions of the Marquis. In the 18th century, Cadzow Castle was rebuilt as a folly and, now owned by Historic Scotland, is situated within the grounds of Chatelherault Country Park not far from the park's magnificent Chatelherault hunting lodge, named after the Duke of Chatelherault (the title bestowed upon James Hamilton by Henry II of France in the 16th century).

Chatelherault was designed in the 1730s by the famous Scottish architect William Adam, who also built Hamilton Old Parish Church in 1734. The church, the only one Adam ever built, is the oldest building in Hamilton still used for its original purpose. Of the other great landmarks commissioned by the Hamilton family only the Mausoleum,

in Strathclyde Park, the family tomb with its 120 feet high dome built in the mid-1800s, still stands. This is said to have the longest echo of any building in the world.

Hamilton Barracks was formerly the Depot of The Cameronians (Scottish Rifles) and the home of the 1st Battalion of the Regiment. The Regimental Museum is part of the Low Parks Museum.

The former Edwardian Town Hall now houses the library and concert hall. The Townhouse complex underwent a sympathetic modernization in 2002 and opened to the public in summer 2004.

During the 17th century Hamilton was the main stopping place for the Scotland to England stagecoach. The Coaching Inn, recently refurbished, is the oldest building in Hamilton and is now the Low Parks Museum on Muir Street. The old route south through Muir Wynd was long recognised as difficult for coaches. To avoid this route a new highway was constructed in 1819 by Thomas Telford which included a bridge over the Cadzow Burn. The commercial heart of the town then shifted to Cadzow Street.

In 1791 Hamilton Parish had just over 5,000 residents but within 100 years that figure had increased by 700% to more than 35,000 due to the cotton and coal industry booms and the opening of the Caledonian Central Railway Station.

With the end of the mining boom and the lack of alternative employment Hamilton was declared a distressed area in 1931. However, a survey carried out in 1948 showed that the face of the town had changed yet again. Large numbers of people in the town were employed in public administration and the professions, some employed locally and others commuting to Glasgow and the surrounding area.

Service industries and local government are now the major employers in Hamilton, as are the financial institution HSBC/First Direct and Philips, the Dutch electronics conglomerate. The town centre has been regenerated over the last decade by creating two new indoor shopping centres and the Palace Grounds Retail Park.

Restaurants and national retail outlets are situated in a redeveloped part of the Palace Grounds that are visible upon entering the town from the M74 motorway. The creation of a circular Town Square has resulted in Hamilton receiving numerous town planning awards during the past decade. This development transformed the Hamilton side of Strathclyde Park, which was the original site of the Duke's palace.

Hamilton Park Racecourse is one of the major Scottish horse racetracks, and Hamilton Academical, the town's football club, is the only professional side in Britain to originate as a school team.

Above Right: Cream House
Below Right: Low Parks Museum
Opposite: Strathclyde Loch.
All unattributed photographs supplied by South Lanarkshire District Council

JAMES, 1ST DUKE OF HAMILTON
1606 – 1649

James, 1st Duke of Hamilton

General Sir James Hamilton, 1st Duke of Hamilton was a Scottish nobleman and influential English Civil war military leader.

The son of James Hamilton, 2nd Marquis of Hamilton, and of the Lady Ann Cunningham, daughter of James Cunningham, 7th Earl of Glencairn, was born on 19 June 1606 at Hamilton Palace, Lanarkshire. Following the death of his insane great-uncle James Hamilton, 3rd Earl of Arran, in 1609 the infant was styled Earl of Arran.

The young James' close ancestor was the Princess Mary, daughter to James II of Scotland and Mary of Gueldres. The fall of the House of Stewart looked increasingly possible after the death of Henry Frederick, Prince of Wales, in 1612. The young Earl of Arran would have become heir to the throne of Scotland should anything have happened to the young Charles, Duke of Rothesay, and his sister Elizabeth.

In 1625 the 2nd Marquis died at Whitehall of a seizure and the new Marquis received all his father's titles. At the coronation of King Charles I of England, Hamilton bore the Sword of State at Westminster Abbey.

From 1631 Hamilton took part in the Thirty Years' War in Germany. His army was destroyed by disease and starvation, and after the complete failure of the expedition Hamilton returned to England in September 1634.

He now became Charles I's chief adviser in Scottish affairs and he was appointed commissioner for Scotland after the outbreak of the revolt against the new Prayer-Book.

During the following three years he travelled between England and Scotland trying, but often failing, to bring the Scottish parliamentary and religious factions under the control of England.

War was now declared, and Hamilton was chosen to command an expedition to the Forth to menace the rear of the Scottish Presbyterian Movement known as The Covenanters. On arrival on 1 May 1639 he found the plan impossible, despaired of success, and was recalled to London in June. On 8 July 1639, after a hostile reception in Edinburgh, he resigned his commission.

On 10 August 1641 Hamilton accompanied Charles I of England on his last visit to Scotland. His aim now was to effect an alliance between the King and Archibald Campbell, 8th Earl of Argyll, and when this failed he abandoned Charles and adhered to Argyll.

Shortly afterwards a plot to seize Argyll, Hamilton and the latter's brother, William Hamilton, Earl of Lanark, was discovered, and on 12 October 1641 they fled from Edinburgh. Hamilton returned not long afterwards and, notwithstanding all that had occurred, still retained Charles' favour and confidence, returning with him to London.

In July 1642 Hamilton went to Scotland on a hopeless mission to prevent the intervention of the Scots in the impending English Civil War, and a breach then took place between him and Argyll.

On 12 April 1643 Hamilton was further ennobled by King Charles at Oxford where he conferred upon the Marquis the titles of Duke of Hamilton, Marquis of Clydesdale, Earl of Cambridge, the Baronies of Aven and Innerdale. In addition he also re-granted the Earldom of Arran.

More political scheming in Scotland resulted in Hamilton having no control over the parliament and so he and Lanark were obliged to leave Scotland, arriving at Oxford on 16 December 1643. Hamilton's conduct had at last incurred Charles' resentment and he was held under house arrest in a house owned by a baker called Daniells with only two servants. In January 1644 he was imprisoned in Pendennis Castle, and the following year moved to St Michael's Mount, where he was liberated by Lord Fairfax's troops on 23 April 1646.

In 1646 Charles I conferred on the Duke the heritable office of Keeper of Holyroodhouse.

Subsequently Hamilton showed great activity in the futile negotiations between the Scots and Charles I at Newcastle. In 1648, in consequence of the seizure of Charles I by the army in 1647, Hamilton obtained a temporary influence and authority in the Scottish parliament over Argyll, and led a large force into England in support of the King on 8 July 1648. He showed complete incapacity in military command and though outnumbering the enemy by 24,000 to about 9,000 men, allowed his troops to disperse over the country and to be defeated by Oliver Cromwell during the three days 17–19 August 1648 at the so-called Battle of Preston. He was himself taken prisoner on 25 August.

Hamilton was tried on 6 February 1649, condemned to death on 6 March and executed by decapitation on 9 March.

Hamilton, during his unfortunate career, had often been suspected of betraying the King's cause, and, as an heir to the Scottish throne, of intentionally playing into the hands of the Covenanters with a view to procuring the crown for himself.

However, his career is sufficiently explained by his thoroughly weak and egotistical character. He took no interest whatsoever in the great questions at issue, was neither loyal nor patriotic, and only desired peace and compromise to avoid personal losses.

The 17th century saw the beginning of the British Empire, firstly in Ireland followed by America and then around the world. Members of the Hamilton clan were obviously among the settlers in these countries and many have given their names to townships, towns and cities along with waterways and mountains. Many of these are celebrated in the following pages.

Ireland

"Geordie's Place" in Hamiltonsbawn. Photograph by J.Jacek

HAMILTONSBAWN, COUNTY ARMAGH, NORTHERN IRELAND, 1619

Hamiltonsbawn or Hamilton's Bawn is a small village in County Armagh, Northern Ireland, five miles east of Armagh. It lies within the Parish of Mullabrack and the Armagh City and District Council area.

The village is named after the fortified house with defended courtyard that was built by Scottish settler John Hamilton, brother of James Hamilton, 1st Viscount Claneboye, in 1619. By 1622 the lime and stone walls of this structure were 12 feet high and 90 feet long by 63 feet broad. It was destroyed during the 1641 Rebellion.

JOHN HAMILTON (1568 – 1639)

The Hamiltons had influential family connections during the Settlement and Plantation. James was the eldest of six brothers, five of whom moved to Ireland. The Hamilton Manuscripts say that the family "abounded in natural affection toward each other". John was born and educated in Scotland, and came to Ulster as brother James' legal advisor. He later purchased large estates around County Armagh (where he and his descendants established Hamiltonsbawn, Newtownhamilton, and Markethill) and also in County Cavan (near Coroneary, Bailieborough and Hansborough). Near the County Armagh lands were the Acheson estates, established by Archibald Acheson, a fellow Scot who had arrived in Ulster from Gosford, East Lothian around 1610, with Scottish families as his new tenants.

John Hamilton is described in The Hamilton Manuscripts as "...a prudent person, and painful man..." He married Sarah Brabazon, daughter of Lord Brabazon of Roscommon, and they had five children. When John Hamilton died he was buried at Mullabrack, Markethill in County Armagh, where Scotsman Robert Mercer had been minister since around 1617. When Sarah Hamilton died a memorial to her was erected inside the church. Reverend Mercer was killed and both the church and monument were destroyed during the 1641 rebellion.

MANORHAMILTON, COUNTY LEITRIM, IRISH REPUBLIC, 1634

Old Church Street, Manorhamilton. Photograph by Dean Molyneaux

Manorhamilton is a small town in north County Leitrim, Ireland. It is located between Sligo and Enniskillen.

Before the Plantations of Ireland, when England confiscated Irish land and gave it to settlers from England and the Scottish lowlands, the settlement was known as Clooneen. This lay on the west bank of the Owenbeg. O'Rourke was the local Gaelic chieftain, based in nearby Dromahair, whose land was seized by the English and then granted to Sir Frederick Hamilton for his services in the European wars of the 17th century. As a result of his actions Hamilton to this day is considered to have been a tyrant by the local people. He began building a new town on the east bank of the river,

Above Left: Main Street, Manorhamilton. Photograph by F.Gertin
Above Centre: Market House, Manorhamilton. Photograph by Whitewoodz
Above Right: Church of Ireland in Manorhamilton. Photograph by Whitewoodz
Opposite: Manorhamilton Castle. Photograph by F.Gertin

in the townland of Clonmullen, which he re-named Manorhamilton. After the town emerged the name Baile Hamaltuin was adopted by Irish speakers and its anglicised form, Ballyhamilton, was used by English speakers for a time.

The ruins of Manorhamilton Castle have recently been impressively renovated transforming it into a fascinating tourist attraction. The Castle was erected in 1634 by Sir Frederick Hamilton. Hamilton was a very unpopular overlord and faced frequent uprisings before the Castle was burned by the Earls of Clanrickard in 1652. Manorhamilton Castle Heritage Centre hosts a permanent exhibition and offers guided tours of the Castle ruins and grounds.

Like most rural Irish towns Manorhamilton is seeing considerable social and physical change. Farming is still a dominant sector but traditional industries and livelihoods are slowly being replaced by new forms of economic activity. Construction in the area recently underwent a boom time with hundreds of new homes having been built. However, the recent recession has brought an end to the building boom.

SIR FREDERICK HAMILTON (1590–1647)

Frederick was the youngest son of Claud Hamilton, 1st Lord Paisley. He was given lands in Leitrim, in the northwest of Ireland in 1622.

Over the next two decades he increased his estate to 18,000 acres and built Manorhamilton Castle around which grew the town of Manorhamilton.

In November 1631 Sir Frederick entered Swedish military service and became colonel of a Scottish-Irish regiment which served in Germany for 15 months. They fought General Tott's army in the Elbe and Weser basins and the Rhineland. After spending a few years back in Leitrim he unsuccessfully attempted to re-enter Swedish military service in September 1637.

During the Irish Rebellion of 1641 Manorhamilton came under constant siege, but the castle remained intact. After the 1643 Cessation Hamilton became a colonel of a regiment of horse in the army of the Solemn League and Covenant in Scotland and Northern England, while still retaining his foot regiment in western Ulster.

In 1642, in punishment for cattle raids by the O'Rourke clan, he sacked the nearby town of Sligo, burning several buildings to the ground, including Sligo Abbey. He then retreated back to Manorhamilton.

Local legend tells that on the way over the mountains to Manorhamilton some of Hamilton's men became lost in heavy fog. A guide on a white horse offered to lead them safely over the mountain, but intentionally led the men over a cliff and to their doom. This legend is the subject of a short story by W. B. Yeats entitled 'The Curse Of The Fires And Of The Shadows'.

In 1647 Sir Frederick left the then disbanding Scottish army and returned to Edinburgh, where he died later that year in relative poverty. He lost all his estates in Ireland, and received very little compensation or financial support from the English parliament for his military efforts. His youngest son Gustavus was raised to the Peerage of Ireland as Viscount Boyne.

Another View of the Castle. Photograph by Whitewoodz

NEWTOWNHAMILTON, COUNTY ARMAGH, NORTHERN IRELAND, 1773

Saint Michael's Chapel, Newtownhamilton. Photograph by Terry Stewart

Newtownhamilton is a small village in County Armagh, Northern Ireland, within the townland of Tullyvallan and the barony of Upper Fews. In the 2001 Census it had a population of 648 people.

The village is built around a narrow Main Street and it hosts a weekly cattle market.

Before the Plantation of Ulster the area of Newtownhamilton was known as Tullyvallan. This is derived either from the Irish Tulaigh Mhalainn, or Tulach Uí Mheallain.

The village takes its name from Alexander Hamilton (1690 – 1768), a descendant of the John Hamilton from Scotland who founded Hamiltonsbawn in 1619. (Not the more famous American, Alexander Hamilton.) The parish was created in 1773 out of the neighbouring parish of Creggan. Some local people refer to the town as 'Newtown'.

In May 1920 Frank Aiken led 200 IRA men in an attack on the Royal Irish Constabulary barracks in Newtownhamilton, the police did not surrender and the IRA retreated.

There were at least nine deaths during 'the troubles' in the 1970's.

HAMILTON'S SEAT, COUNTY ANTRIM, NORTHERN IRELAND, 1786

Site of Hamilton's Seat. Photograph by Anne Burgess

You would expect this feature named on the OS map to be a rock formation, but it turns out that it is in fact a seat! It is at a viewpoint on the west side of Benbane Head. The trace of the lower path, now closed, can be seen climbing from below the columnar basalt through the red lateritic layer and scree to reach the top of the cliff by a set of rough steps, now blocked off. Hamilton's Seat is just beside the top of the path. It was named after the Reverend Doctor William Hamilton, who in 1786 was the first to publish an accurate description of the geology here.

Other Hamiltons in Ireland

Mount Hamilton – County Tyrone. Photograph by Terry Allen

MOUNT HAMILTON, COUNTY TYRONE, NORTHERN IRELAND

A township in County Tyrone

MOUNT HAMILTON, COUNTY ANTRIM, NORTHERN IRELAND

A township in County Antrim

The United States Of America

HAMILTONBAN, ADAMS COUNTY, PENNSYLVANIA, 1749

Hamiltonban Township is in Adams County, Pennsylvania. The township, with a population about 2,500, is named after Hamiltonsbawn in County Armagh, Northern Ireland.

The earliest European settlers came to the area in the 1730s. They were mostly Scotch-Irish who came to America to escape famine in Ireland. In the early days parts of what are now Adams and York Counties were claimed by both Maryland and Pennsylvania. One such area was "Carroll's Delight" which was chartered in 1735 by Maryland, and covered 5,000 acres in the vicinity of Fairfield and Hamiltonban. The Pennsylvania Provincial Assembly created York County in 1749, which included all of what is now Adams County. The 1749 charter created "Hamilton's Bann" township, which then covered what are now Hamiltonban, Liberty and Freedom Townships as well as Fairfield and Carroll Valley Boroughs.

The early years were difficult for the settlers, especially during the war between the British and French for control of North America. Most of the local Native American Indians sided with the French, and the early Pennsylvania settlers in frontier areas like Hamiltonban were repeatedly raided by the Indians, and much bloodshed resulted. After the war most of the Indians retreated westward and the area was calm again, although still in dispute by Pennsylvania and Maryland. Ownership was finally settled in 1767 with the surveying of the Mason-Dixon Line. By that time people of German descent were settling in the area, and they came to dominate local politics before 1800.

The largest settlement in Hamiltonban, Fairfield, was laid out on 247 acres of land in Carroll's Delight purchased by John Miller in 1755. Squire Miller quickly sold off lots for the purpose of agriculture, built a stone manor house in 1757, and licensed it as a tavern in 1786. This stone house, now called the Fairfield Inn, is still in use as a tavern. In 1800 Adams County was formed from York County and Hamiltonban Township became part of Adams County. In 1801 William Miller, John Miller's son, had his land surveyed and platted for a town to be known as Millerstown. When it was learned that a town by that name already existed the name was changed to Fairfield.

Throughout the nineteenth century Fairfield was part of Hamiltonban Township. By far the most traumatic event of this century in Adams County was the Battle of Gettysburg which took place during the American Civil War (1861-1865) and was the most deadly battle ever to take place on American soil. This ultimate and decisive confrontation between North and South, and between two ways of life, marked the high water mark of the Confederate tide. Located just south of the focal point of the battle, Fairfield most definitely felt the reverberations.

Early in the day on July 3rd, 1863, Jones' Brigade of Stewart's Cavalry Division of the Confederate Army of Northern Virginia fought a bloody battle with the 6th U.S. Cavalry on Carroll's Tract Road, just 2 miles north of Fairfield. The Union Cavalry was driven back to Emmitsburg, and Jones' Brigade remained in Fairfield, protecting the left flank of the Confederate Army during Pickett's Charge on the decisive day of the Battle of Gettysburg. Jones' Brigade encamped at Fairfield that night, and the next day one of two major columns of the Army of Northern Virginia began their retreat through Fairfield, up Iron Springs Road, and over South Mountain through Monterey Gap. The other column, with Lee's wagons, supplies, and wounded, retreated through Cashtown towards Chambersburg.

In 1896 Fairfield was incorporated as a borough, with its own governing body separate from Hamiltonban. Carroll Valley Borough was chartered from Hamiltonban and Liberty Townships on September 30, 1974.

Opposite: Fairfield Inn in Fairfield, once part of Hamiltonban. Robert E. Lee stayed here. Photograph by Acroterion

HAMILTON TOWNSHIP, FRANKLIN COUNTY, PENNSYLVANIA, 1752

Old House and Barn on Historic Lincoln Highway. Photograph by M. Wolford

Vintage Texaco Gas Pump. Photograph by M. Wolford

Hamilton Township was founded in 1752 and was named in honour of James Hamilton, Governor of Pennsylvania at various times from 1748 to 1773.

The township is rich in historical lore, and during colonial days was the scene of many stirring events. In 1755 the settlers defended themselves against the Native American Indians. No military system existed at the time and forts were built to defend the frontier against the Indians. One of these forts, Fort McCord, was erected in 1755 but was attacked and burned in April 1756. A number of people were killed and a marker stands on Fort McCord Road identifying the site of this tragedy.

A decade of growth followed and when the Revolution started a company of men

from the region joined Washington at the siege of Boston in August 1775 and in the campaigns of the following two years. When the war moved to the southern colonies life returned to normal and farming continued to be the principal industry, although a number of sawmills and gristmills also provided employment.

By 1840 nearly 2,000 people lived in the Township but peace was not to remain for long. The Civil War saw men enlist, normally for 3 years in the Pennsylvania Volunteers starting in April 1861, and they were involved in a number of battles including Gettysburg.

Hamilton Township remained very much a rural community throughout the 20th

Roadside Giant. Photograph by M. Wolford

century, emerging from the depression and the 2nd World War still very much an agricultural community. There is now a major emphasis on dairy farming, and there are also orchards and sawmills in the Township area.

The fifth and final project in the "Roadside Giants of the Lincoln Highway" series is an antique truck celebrating farming heritage. Designed by the Franklin County Career & Technology Centre students in Chambersburg, the 1920 Selden Apple Truck replica truck is fully dimensional and features a steering column and bench seat plus wheels that spin. The 11-foot tall, 2-ton antique truck is located at Shatzer's Fruit Market along U.S. 30 heading east.

Roadside fruit stands were bountiful in the early Lincoln Highway days, and Franklin County still has a strong connection to agriculture. While it was easy to choose a vintage apple truck to replicate, it is the most complex of all of the designs.

JAMES HAMILTON (1710 – 1783)

James Hamilton, son of the well-known Philadelphia lawyer Andrew Hamilton, was a prominent lawyer and governmental figure in colonial Philadelphia and Pennsylvania. Hamilton was educated in Philadelphia and England before becoming a practising lawyer in 1731. When on December 28, 1733 his father resigned as principal clerk of the supreme court of Pennsylvania, James was appointed to the office.

In May 1734 James' father, Andrew Hamilton, sold him the town site of Lancaster, Pennsylvania for the price of five shillings. Later that month, on May 21, James secured a patent from the Penn family for his grant on the Lancaster land. After the death of Andrew Hamilton on August 4, 1741, James Hamilton assisted his brother-in-law, William Allen, in the administration of lands purchased by his father to be used for the state house and surrounding public space. He was elected to the provincial assembly in 1745 and was re-elected five times. James served as mayor of Philadelphia for one year from October 1745.

Hamilton became a member of the provincial council in 1746, and was commissioned by the sons of William Penn as lieutenant-governor. He served in this capacity until 1754, then again from 1759 to 1763, then briefly also in 1771 and 1773.

HAMILTON TOWNSHIP, MONROE COUNTY, PENNSYLVANIA, 1762

Hamilton Township was created on December 24, 1762 and is the second-oldest township in Monroe County. Originally formed by the Northampton County court, Hamilton Township was most likely named in honour of James Hamilton, the then lieutenant governor of Pennsylvania.

The earliest deed recorded in Hamilton Township was between the Penn family and Nicholas Weiser of Bucks County for 244 acres. This tract of land was shortly thereafter sold to Richard Peters, who sold the land to John McDowell in 1764. McDowell, an immigrant from Northern Ireland, had lived with the Nicholas DePui family in Smithfield Township when he first arrived in the area. McDowell eventually married one of DePui's daughters.

The earliest road in the township was the Sullivan Road, part of the route that General John Sullivan had taken northward during his famed "march" in 1778 to the Wyoming Valley. In June 1779, General John Sullivan was ordered to march north through Pennsylvania into New York to "subdue" and "punish" the native Iroquois Indians. The Iroquois were at that time allies with the British and had organized various raids in the northern frontier against the new nation. Sullivan and his army of 2,000 men began their march in Easton and after two days of marching reached Sciota and Brinker's Mill in Hamilton Township; here, Sullivan secured supplies and provisions for his troops.

The first school was constructed of logs and was located near the Hamilton Church. John Adam Eyer, a popular schoolmaster, taught there in German, and was paid 50 cents per student per month for his work.

The Christ Hamilton United Lutheran Church in Sciota is referred to as the "Mother Church" of Lutheran churches in Monroe County. The history of the congregation dates to 1755, and the first headstone in the church's cemetery dates to 1778. The cornerstone of the church was laid on May 28, 1829, and the church was officially dedicated on November 6-7, 1830. Sermons were delivered in German through the

1850s. The township's oldest burial ground is also associated with the Christ Church.

Within the township Kellersville was ideally located on the Easton-Belmont Turnpike, another early road, which connected directly to Easton, Pennsylvania, the county seat of Northampton County, and eventually to Philadelphia. John George Keller was a landowner and businessman in Kellersville who built a well-placed grist mill along the highly-travelled turnpike. Kellersville also boasted a church, a tavern, a school house, a store, and many residential dwellings. As Kellersville was centrally located in the county and had a large road into Easton, many citizens believed Kellersville would serve as a natural seat for the newly-formed county.

Daniel Stroud, son of town-founder Jacob Stroud, was responsible for the general development of Stroudsburg. Stroudsburg was nestled within three natural water boundaries: Brodhead Creek to the east; McMichaels Creek to the south, and Pocono Creek to the west. Daniel was inspired by the well-planned small towns and communities of New England. He was responsible not only for laying out wide and shaded downtown streets, but for obtaining a charter to designate Stroudsburg as a borough in 1815, separating it from Smithfield Township.

A special election was held, but the voting was filled with deception, fraud, and misrepresentation. It was well-known that 14-year-old boys, too young to vote, had cast ballots. It was also discovered that names on the election lists were fictitious and that many of the voters resided in the cemetery, their names having been taken from the moss-covered tombstones. The total number of votes for both towns was 2,194 — 402 more adult men than were living in Monroe County at that time. Unfortunately for Kellersville of Hamilton Township, local politics played too great a role, and the fraudulent voting was upheld in the local court.

Stroudsburg was chosen as the government seat of the newly-formed Monroe County, Pennsylvania. The ruling by the early court system ended the legal proceedings, but not the debate regarding which town should have been chosen as the seat for the newly-formed Monroe County. During the early days of Hamilton Township agriculture was the inhabitants' main occupation as the limestone ridges provided fertile soil for farm fields. The staple farming products in the 1880's were grains, corn, potatoes, hay, and fruits, including apples, pears, and plums. It was reported that peaches could "attain great perfection" in some regions of the township.

In 1840, the census reported that 1,508 individuals lived in Monroe County. One hundred years later, the population was 1,665. In 2000, the population of Hamilton Township was 8,235 people.

Text by Amy Leiser
Above Left: Cherry Valley Methodist Church. Photograph by Kim Williams
Above Centre: Footbridge in Rural Hamilton Township.
Photograph by Kim Williams
Above Right: One Roomed Schoolhouse. Photograph by Kim Williams

Hamilton Vista. Photograph by Nicholas

FORT HAMILTON, RHODE ISLAND, 1780

Rose Island Light from the South. Photograph by Julian Colton

Fort Hamilton Historic District includes all of Rose Island in Newport, Rhode Island. The district includes Rose Island Light and an early U.S. military fortification designed in part by Major Louis de Tousard. The fort was named after Alexander Hamilton.

The earliest fortifications on Rose Island were built in 1780, during the American Revolution, around the time of the Battle of Rhode Island. Later construction took place from 1798 to 1801 but was left largely unfinished, except for a long barracks building used by the U.S. Infantry. In the 19th century Fort Hamilton was used as a quarantine station for the port of Newport, and the island served as a popular picnic destination. Starting in the late 19th century, the island became part of the U.S. Naval Torpedo Station, and during World War I and World War II the fort was used for munitions storage by the U.S. Navy as it conducted torpedo tests. During World War II anti-aircraft guns were also added to the island. The fort was added to the National Register of Historic Places in 2001.

ALEXANDER HAMILTON (1755 OR 1757 – 1804)

Alexander Hamilton was a Founding Father, soldier, economist, political philosopher, one of America's first constitutional lawyers and the first United States Secretary of the Treasury.

Of illegitimate birth and raised in the West Indies, Hamilton was effectively orphaned at about the age of 11. Recognized for his abilities and talent, he went to North America for his education, sponsored by people from his community. He attended King's College (now Columbia University).

Hamilton served in the American Revolutionary War. At the start of the war he organized an artillery company and was chosen as its captain. He later became the senior aide-de-camp and confidant to General George Washington, the American Commander-in-Chief. After the American Revolutionary War, Hamilton was elected to the Continental Congress representing New York. He resigned to practise law, and founded the Bank of New York. Hamilton was among those dissatisfied with the first national governance document, the Articles of Confederation. While serving in the New York Legislature, Hamilton was sent as a delegate to the Annapolis Convention in 1786 to revise the Articles, but it resulted in a call for a new constitution instead. He was one of New York's delegates at the Philadelphia Convention that drafted the new constitution in 1787, and was the only New Yorker who signed it. In support of ratification by the states for the new Constitution, Hamilton wrote many of the Federalist Papers, still an important source for Constitutional interpretation. He served again under Washington in the army raised to defeat the Whiskey Rebellion, a tax revolt of western farmers in 1794. In 1798 Hamilton called for mobilization against France after the XYZ Affair, and secured an appointment as commander of a new army, which he trained for war. However, the Quasi-War, although hard-fought at sea, was never officially declared. In the end President John Adams found a diplomatic solution that avoided war.

In the new government under President George Washington, Hamilton was appointed the Secretary of the Treasury. As Secretary of the Treasury, he was the primary author of the economic policies of the George Washington Administration, especially the funding of the state debts by the Federal government, the establishment of a national bank, a system of tariffs, and friendly trade relations with Britain. An admirer of British political systems, Hamilton was a nationalist who emphasized strong central government, and successfully argued that the implied powers of the Constitution could be used to fund the national debt, assume state debts, and create the government-owned Bank of the United States. These programmes were funded primarily by a tariff on imports and later also by a highly controversial excise tax on whiskey.

Embarrassed when an extra-marital affair with Maria Reynolds became public, Hamilton resigned from office in 1795 and returned to practise law in New York. However, he kept his hand in politics and was a powerful influence on the cabinet of President Adams (1797–1801). Hamilton's opposition to John Adams helped cause Adams' defeat in the 1800 elections. When Thomas Jefferson and Aaron Burr tied in the Electoral College, Hamilton helped defeat his bitter personal enemy Burr and elect Jefferson as president. After opposing Adams, the candidate of his own party, Hamilton was left with few political friends. In 1804, as the next presidential election approached, Hamilton again opposed the candidacy of Burr. Taking offence at some of his comments, Burr challenged him to a duel and mortally wounded Hamilton, who died within days.

Alexander Hamilton

HAMILTON COUNTY, OHIO, 1790

Hamilton County, Ohio, was established on January 2, 1790. It was the second county formed in the Northwest Territory. Residents named the county in honour of Alexander Hamilton, who was the First Secretary of the Treasury of the United States. Located in the south western corner of Ohio, the county's southern border helps form Ohio's boundary with Kentucky, while its western border helps form the state's boundary with Indiana. Cincinnati is the county's largest city and the county seat.

In 1788 Israel Ludlow, Matthias Denman, and Robert Patterson purchased eight hundred acres in Ohio from John Cleves Symmes across the Ohio River from the mouth of the Licking River. Symmes had purchased two million acres of land from the United States in 1787 and now hoped to become rich by selling parts of the Symmes Purchase to others. Denman provided the necessary cash; Patterson found settlers; and Ludlow surveyed the land to make sales and also to establish a town. By early January 1789, Ludlow had platted the town, dividing it into two types of lots. Near the town's centre lots were one-half acre in size while outlying lots were four acres. Ludlow, Denman, and Patterson provided the first thirty settlers with two free lots, one of each type. The three men named the town Losantiville. The name of the town was a concoction of terms loosely meaning that this was a 'city across from the mouth of the Licking River'.

The town and the surrounding countryside grew slowly. One month after the men established the settlement only three log cabins existed in Losantiville. On the outlying lots settlers had constructed twenty cabins and one frame house. Eleven families and two dozen single men lived on the land. In August 1789 the village began to grow quickly. In that month, Josiah Harmar authorized the construction of Fort Washington to protect settlers in both the Symmes Purchase and the Miami Purchase, as well as in northern Kentucky. The fort was located just west of Denman's, Ludlow's, and Patterson's eight hundred acres of land. When it was completed in December 1789, Harmar made Fort Washington his headquarters. Usually three hundred soldiers lived in the fort, increasing Losantiville's population to nearly five hundred people. In 1790 the governor of the Northwest Territory, Arthur St. Clair, proceeded to establish Hamilton County and made Losantiville the county seat. St. Clair disliked the name Losantiville and changed the town's name to Cincinnati. An additional 250 families arrived later that year, swelling the town's population to nearly seven hundred people.

Law and order remained absent from Hamilton County during its early years. The settlers organized a court and hired a sheriff, but the soldiers routinely had to establish martial law in the area. This became especially common as tensions increased with the local Native Americans, especially the Shawnee Indians. Contributing to the lawlessness many residents grew corn, which they distilled into alcohol and sold to the soldiers. During 1790 and 1791, thousands of militiamen from Kentucky and Pennsylvania flooded Cincinnati as Harmar and eventually St. Clair planned expeditions against the Indians. St. Clair faced such a difficult time maintaining control of his men in Cincinnati, with its three taverns, that he moved his men to nearby Ludlow's Station.

After St. Clair's defeat at the hands of the Indians in 1791, many settlers fled Hamilton County, fearing that the native Indians would descend upon them. Despite the lack of order and the various safety concerns, hundreds of settlers continued to come to the region. They believed that they could make their fortunes providing the soldiers and people travelling down the Ohio River with supplies. By the summer of 1792 thirty warehouses existed in Cincinnati to meet these needs. With the success of Anthony Wayne against the Indians at the Battle of Fallen Timbers in 1794 more settlers arrived in Hamilton County. In 1803, the year that the United States Army abandoned Fort Washington, the county had roughly two thousand civilian residents. It continued to grow, reaching nearly fifteen thousand people by 1820.

During the nineteenth century Hamilton County villages, especially Cincinnati,

Cincinnati in 1841

continued to grow. The Ohio River provided residents with numerous business opportunities. Hotels, restaurants, and taverns quickly opened to meet the needs of settlers travelling westward on the Ohio River. Steamboats were manufactured and repaired in Cincinnati. Farmers brought their crops to Hamilton County to send down the Ohio and Mississippi Rivers to New Orleans, Louisiana, one of Ohio's major markets. The Miami and Erie Canal made the trip from western Ohio to the Ohio River much easier and less expensive for local farmers. In the early 1800s Cincinnati developed into an important meatpacking centre. Farmers brought their livestock to the city where it was then slaughtered, processed, and sold to western settlers or shipped to various markets. Due to Cincinnati's association with meatpacking, the city became known as the "Porkopolis" of the United States.

Hamilton County also played an important role in the intellectual and cultural development of Ohio during the first half of the nineteenth century. In 1819 Daniel Drake established the Medical College of Ohio, hoping to improve medical care on the frontier. Numerous literary figures including Harriet Beecher Stowe, the author of Uncle Tom's Cabin, called the county home for at least part of their lives. Americans from both the North and the South settled in the community, creating a very diverse and worldly population.

Cincinnatus Statue. Photograph by R Dikeman
Opposite: The Cincinnati Skyline at night. Photograph by D Jensen

Roebling Bridge and City Skyline. Photograph by Nicole Haake

The Belle of Louiseville Docks in Cincinnati. Photograph by Bryce Mullet

Some residents opposed the activities of other people in the county and actively campaigned to reform their neighbours. The temperance movement targeted the Germans and the Irish, who were alleged to be well known for their supposedly heavy drinking. Ohio abolitionists campaigned against slavery. Located directly across the Ohio River from Kentucky, a slaveholding state, Hamilton County abolitionists published newspapers and anti-slavery tracts, hoping to convince their slaveholding neighbours to free their slaves. Participants in the Underground Railroad also smuggled runaway slaves across the Ohio River to possible freedom in the North. Not all Ohioans supported the abolitionists. Many of these people feared that, if slavery ended, they would face competition from the freed African Americans. Race riots sometimes occurred, especially when some whites feared that African Americans were gaining too much power or were infringing upon their opportunities. In 1829, one such riot occurred in Cincinnati, because Irish immigrants disliked competition from the African-American community.

During the American Civil War, most residents supported the United States, but a sizable number of people went to the South to fight for the Confederacy. Hamilton County served as a major recruiting and training centre for the United States military during the Civil War. Businesses and farmers thrived, as they provided supplies to the soldiers and housing for both the soldiers and their families.

By the late 1880s, Cincinnati was the largest city in Ohio, with almost 300,000 people. At this time Cincinnati had the densest population of any city in the United States. More than fifteen railroads connected Cincinnati to other parts of the United States. The major industry in Hamilton County was iron production, followed closely by meatpacking, cloth production, and woodworking. An art museum and art academy existed in Cincinnati, as well as an opera house and the Music Hall and Exposition Building. The University of Cincinnati provided residents with access to a college education. Hamilton County also played a major role in Ohio government.

For most of the twentieth century, Hamilton County experienced continued growth both culturally and economically. Surprisingly, Cincinnati's population has remained relatively constant since the 1880s with its population in 2000 at 365,000 people. Hamilton County then contained 845,303 people.

Today many major corporations operate in Cincinnati and a number have their national or regional headquarters located there. County residents enjoy diverse employment opportunities. This diversity has helped people to weather economic downturns comparatively easily, as no single business employs more than three per cent of the county's workforce.

In the early 2000s, Hamilton County remains the cultural centre of south western Ohio, northern Kentucky, and southern Indiana. The county boasts two major professional sports franchises, the Cincinnati Reds and the Cincinnati Bengals. Numerous theatres operate in the county, including the Cincinnati College Conservatory of Music, and Music Hall. More than one hundred art galleries exist in Cincinnati and the surrounding area. The Cincinnati Zoo and Botanical Garden is known for its successful breeding programmes.

Despite this tremendous cultural and economic growth, not all residents are able to enjoy the benefits of living within Hamilton County's borders. Some residents enjoy life in upscale communities, but many residents live in lower-income areas, including Over-the-Rhine and the Laurel Homes, the largest public housing project in the United States. Many downtown businesses moved from Cincinnati to the suburbs beginning in the 1950s, and wealthier residents went with them. Residents who could not afford to move with the companies experienced a shortage of jobs. This made it difficult for some people to experience the county's numerous benefits. In recent years, Cincinnati officials have made dramatic efforts to revitalize the downtown area, providing local residents with additional opportunities.

Above Right: Cincinnati Reds. Photograph by R Dikeman
Below Right: The Scripps Center. Photograph by Derek Jensen

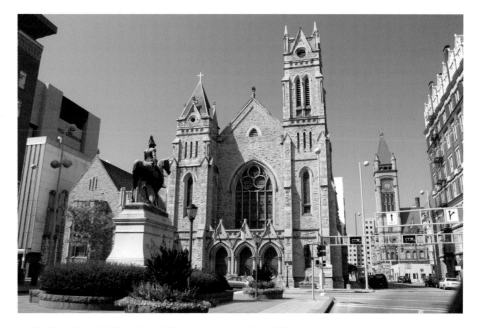

Left: Cincinnati City Hall. Photograph by Paul Hildebrandt
Above: Covenant First Presbyterian Church, Cincinnati.
Photograph by Paul Hildebrandt
Opposite: Union Terminal. Photograph by Paul Hildebrandt

HAMILTON, BUTLER COUNTY, OHIO, 1791

The City of Hamilton, the County Seat of Butler County, is an important regional centre of business, industry, culture, and government. Located in Southwest Ohio, the City of Hamilton is centrally located between the Cincinnati and Dayton metropolitan areas.

Hamilton, Ohio was founded by European Americans in 1791 as Fort Hamilton and was named to honour Alexander Hamilton.

It was a frontier military fort intended primarily as a supply station for the troops of Generals Arthur St. Clair and later Anthony Wayne. Their armies entered the Miami Valley wilderness to drive out the Shawnee and Miami during the Northwest Indian War. The Indians hoped to maintain their territory here, and, following the American Revolutionary War, the United States wanted to open it for other settlement.

The fort was located on the Great Miami River, where the east and west banks rose gradually. The river was ideal for settlement since it is shallow with a gravelly bottom during normal flow and easily forded by men, animals and wagons. By 1800 the fort had been abandoned, and Hamilton was becoming an agricultural and regional trading town. The town was platted, government was seated, and the town named by 1803.

Hamilton was first incorporated by an act of the Ohio General Assembly in 1810, but lost its status in 1815 for failure to hold elections. It was reincorporated in 1827 with Rossville, the community across the Great Miami River in St. Clair Township. The two places severed their connection in 1831 only to be re-joined in 1854. It became a city in 1857. On March 14, 1867, Hamilton withdrew from the townships of Fairfield and St. Clair to form a "paper township", but the city government was dominant.

On the afternoon of September 17, 1859, Abraham Lincoln arrived at the Hamilton station (the station is on the city's Historic Preservation list). He gave a campaign speech in support of his fellow Republican, William Dennison, who was running for Ohio governor. Lincoln's speech concentrated on popular sovereignty. He began "This beautiful and far-famed Miami Valley is the garden spot of the world." It was during this campaign that the relatively unknown Lincoln was first mentioned as a possible presidential contender.

Butler County Courthouse, Hamilton

View of Hamilton Skyline

By the mid-19th century Hamilton had become a significant manufacturing city. Its early products were often machines and equipment used to process the region's farm produce, such as steam engines, hay cutters, reapers, and threshers. Other production included machine tools, house hardware, saws for mills, paper, paper-producing machinery, carriages, guns, whisky, beer, woollen goods, and a myriad and diverse output made from metal, grain, and cloth. By the 20th century, the town was a manufacturing centre for vaults and safes, machine tools, cans for vegetables, paper, paper-producing machinery, locomotives, frogs and switches for railroads, steam engines, diesel engines, foundry products, printing presses, automobile parts, war material, Liberty ship engines, and gun lathes. Manufacturers used coke to feed furnaces. Its by-product, gas, fuelled street lights. The Great Miami River valley, in which Hamilton was located, was an industrial giant.

The county courthouse, listed on the National Register of Historic Places because of its monumental architecture, was constructed between 1885 and 1889. The city has three historic districts, including areas of turn-of-the-century homes. Like Cincinnati, Hamilton had many German and Italian immigrants, whose influence showed in culture, architecture and food. Hamilton also had a Jewish community; Beth Israel Synagogue was founded in 1901 as an Orthodox alternative to Hamilton's existing Reform Synagogue.

In the 1920s, many Chicago gangsters had second homes in Hamilton. This gave Hamilton the nickname "Little Chicago". Some appeared to have invested in what became an active district of gambling and prostitution.

During World War II, the entire city was declared off-limits to military personnel because of its numerous gambling and prostitution establishments. Madame Freeze's and the long row of prostitution houses along Wood Street (now called Pershing Ave) were notorious among soldiers. Factories in Hamilton manufactured military supplies, such as tank turrets, Liberty ship and submarine engines, and machined and stamped metal parts.

On May 28, 1986, as part of a plan to increase publicity about Hamilton, the city council voted 5-1 in favour of adding an exclamation point to the city's name. Thus, Hamilton officially became Hamilton! While used extensively in the city's documents, letterheads, business cards and on local signage, "Hamilton!" was not successful in getting Rand McNally to use the new moniker on state maps. The city no longer uses the exclamation point in marketing materials, correspondence, or local signage.

Above: Hamilton Street Scene
Below: Entrance to German Historic District. Photograph by G Hume

The city has become known for its support of the arts, especially public sculpture. On August 16, 2000, Ohio's Governor Bob Taft declared and formally recognized Hamilton as "the City of Sculpture". This sparked a vision for a group of community members who officially formed Hamilton, Ohio City of Sculpture, Inc.. This organization has been successful at adding many new sculptures in public spaces around Hamilton.

Miami University Hamilton (MUH), a branch campus of Miami University in Oxford, Ohio, was established in 1968. MUH is the largest of Miami's three branch campuses with over 5,000 in enrolment.

Hamilton grew almost 3 per cent from 2000 to 2010, with the 2010 Census reporting a population of 62,477. Unique to a city of this size, the City of Hamilton owns and operates the four primary utility services within the City: electric, natural gas, water and wastewater. Each service is a separate entity from general government operations. Approximately 30,000 customers are served by the utilities. Hamilton has operated the electric utility since 1893 and it is the second largest city owned electric utility in the state. The City both produces and purchases electric power. Hamilton has operated the natural gas utility since 1890. It is the largest city owned gas distribution utility in the state of Ohio. Hamilton has operated the water utility since 1884. The water system is supplied through two well fields that draw from the Great Miami River Valley Aquifer. The city has won the Berkeley Springs International Water Tasting Awards for best-tasting municipal water for the United States in 2009; and the best in the World, Gold Medal, in 2010.

The City of Hamilton continues to evolve from a former manufacturing focused economy to a more diversified economy, with a new strategic plan recently adopted by City Council, which includes a vision statement of "A purposeful destination for working, living and playing". With big city amenities and small town charm, Hamilton continues to retain the character of the city's past while sharpening its focus on a bright, prosperous future.

Text: Stacey Dietrichs
Above Right: Lane Hooven House, one of Hamilton's Historic Buildings.
Photograph by G.Hume
Below Right: New High Street Bridge. Photograph by rflick

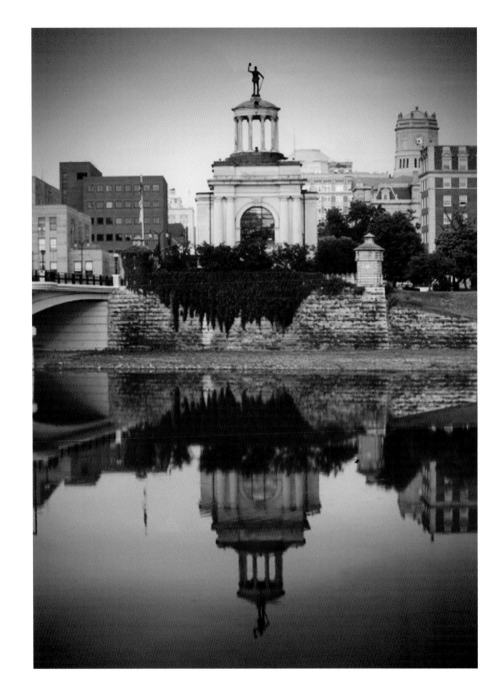

Left: Soldiers and Sailors Memorial reflected in the Miami River
Above: One of Hamilton's many statues
All unattributed Photographs supplied by City of Hamilton Economic
Development Department

HAMILTON, MASSACHUSETTS, 1793

Hamilton Town Hall

Entrance to Myopia Hunt Club. Photograph by John Phelan

Hamilton is a town located in the eastern central portion of Essex County in eastern Massachusetts. Hamilton today is mainly a residential community enjoyed for its lovely views, horse riding trails and close proximity to the many beaches on the North Shore of Boston.

The town of Hamilton is known for its New England charm and the beauty of its fields. The town includes many historic houses and pastoral landscapes. It also has a rich equestrian heritage, which remains strong today due to the influence of the many horse farms and of Myopia Hunt Club, which holds frequent equestrian events, including Polo most Sunday afternoons (and is noted also for its golf course where the US Open was held four times in the early years of the event). The visitor to Hamilton may well share the secondary roads with horseback riders.

Hamilton is closely tied to its sister town, Wenham, sharing a school system, library, recreation department and commuter rail station. In 2010, the community of Hamilton-Wenham was listed among the "Best Places to Live" by Boston Magazine.

In June, 1638, John Winthrop, Jr., son of the founder of the Massachusetts Bay Colony, bought most of present-day Essex County from Masconomet, chief of the Agawam Indians, for the sum of twenty English pounds. A memorial stone on Sagamore Hill in southeastern Hamilton marks where Masconomet was buried with his gun and tomahawk around 1658.

Congregational Church which was at centre of the original 'Hamlet'

Above: Appleton Farm. Photograph supplied by Dhasson at en.wikipedia

Hamilton was first settled in 1638 and was originally a section of Ipswich known as "The Hamlet." The first recorded land grant in the Hamlet was Matthew Whipple's farm, dated 1638. Three years later the new stagecoach road from Boston to Newburyport (Bay Road) was laid out through the Whipple land. Other early settlers of the Hamlet, including the Appletons, Winthrops, Lamsons, and Dodges, were attracted by countryside similar to the English farms and estates they had left behind.

The town was incorporated on June 21, 1793, and named for Alexander Hamilton, whose portrait became the town seal in 1903.

In 1793 Hamilton, then known as "The Hamlet" voted to separate from Ipswich, mainly due to the effort of their then Minister Manasseh Cutler. Cutler was a close friend and admirer of Alexander Hamilton, First Secretary of the Treasury in the new United States Government. He suggested the town be called Hamilton and the name was approved. It is not known if Hamilton ever visited his namesake but he was a frequent visitor at the farm of Timothy Pickering, Washington's Secretary of State, in nearby Wenham where he planted 13 oak trees, for the thirteen original colonies, which still stand.

With the arrival of the Boston and Maine Railroad in 1839, the population centre moved gradually southward toward the depot.

The farm village proved to be an attractive location for Boston groups seeking land for recreation and renewal. A Methodist Ministers' association first held a camp meeting at Asbury Grove in 1859. In the 1880s, the Myopia Hunt Club, which had been named in jest for its near-sighted founders, moved from Winchester, Massachusetts to the Gibney Farm in Hamilton. Beginning as a lawn tennis and baseball club, it turned to polo, the hunt, and golf as members built large summer estates in the area. Myopia donated the site for the General George S. Patton Memorial Park to the town of Hamilton (Hamilton was the home of General George Patton). The park continues to be a recreation centre for the town today.

In 1921 the Mandell family built the Community House in memory of the eight men in Hamilton and Wenham who died in military service during World War I, including their son, Sam. They commissioned Guy Lowell, a respected architect of Boston and New York, to design the building, and gave the Community House in trust for the use of the residents of both towns. Although in its early days the Community House offered activities such as bowling and a men's smoking room, it now features a wide range of classes and activities for all ages.

Hamilton is a fun town to visit with lots of early American History available in nearby Salem, Beverly and Marblehead.

Above Right: L B Bates Memorial Library in Asbury Grove. Photograph by John Phelan
Below Right: Patton's Tank in the George S Patton Memorial Park
Unattributed photographs and some text by Tim Clark

HAMILTON, MARTIN COUNTY, NORTH CAROLINA, 1804

With a modest population of 465, the small town of Hamilton, North Carolina makes up for its small size by being an undeniably historic community. Nestled along the Roanoke River, Hamilton has long enjoyed the privilege of being situated in a prime location surrounded by rich farm and wood lands as well as the diverse plant and animal life that the river fosters.

Incorporated in 1804 this vibrant little settlement, originally known as Milton, was renamed Hamilton in honour of former US Secretary of the Treasury, Alexander Hamilton. Like many other towns in North Carolina in the early nineteenth century, Hamilton owed its early development to its location on a major waterway. Shallow-draft steamboats, a cotton gin and a burgeoning textile trade both at home and abroad brought river traffic to its peak during the years preceding the Civil War.

Hamilton's nationally recognized historic district is a prized asset of which the local community takes great pride. This district includes some of the finest antebellum homes assembled in Martin County. Among the noted sites featured within Hamilton's National Register of Historic Places District are St. Martin's Episcopal Church (circa 1880) and the Hamilton Coloured (Rosenwald) School (circa 1918) as well as a host of other historic houses and buildings.

St. Martin's Episcopal Church was originally established as a missionary station in 1868. The founding of this church is attributed largely to the Boyle family who moved to Hamilton during the Civil War. Today this church stands as a remarkably unaltered and sophisticated example of the Gothic Revival frame church from the early post - Civil War period. It is one of the most outstanding examples of frame Gothic architecture in Eastern North Carolina.

The Hamilton Historic Commission oversees the preservation, maintenance and meaningful use of St. Martin's in cooperation with the Episcopal Diocese of East Carolina. The Commission sponsors an annual Christmas service in the church and the building is open by appointment. In November of 2006, two beautiful commissioned panels by artist David Hewson were installed in St. Martin's.

Right: St. Martin's Episcopal Church (1880). Photograph by Carol Jones Shields

Another point of interest in town, the old Hamilton Coloured School - is one of the famed early Rosenwald Schools. Collectively, Rosenwald Schools were historically black schools built from 1913 to 1932 as a result of the fruitful collaboration that developed between philanthropist, Julius Rosenwald, and Booker T. Washington, educator and founder of the Tuskegee Institute.

The Rosenwald Fund provided supplemental funds for the construction of over 5,000 rural schools to educate black children across the Southeastern United States. Only a precious few survive today. Those that remain have been earmarked as "endangered historic sites" by the National Trust for Historic Preservation.

Recently, the Hamilton community has been working in conjunction with Roanoke River Partners, Inc. to renovate and preserve both this historic site and its culturally rich legacy. Upon completion, the Rosenwald River Centre (the new name) will be repurposed as an interpretive site to tell the "Rosenwald Story" as well as a visitor/community centre for gatherings and eco-tourism ventures. In its new life, this historic site will contribute to both local and regional economies.

Just outside of Hamilton is Fort Branch, an earthen Confederate fort perched on the high bank of the Roanoke. This preserved fort hosts re-enactments and houses a treasure trove of American Civil War history.

At the heart of Hamilton's early development, the Roanoke River remains an economic generator for Hamilton and the larger region. Today, the Hamilton waterfront is a prime recreational resource with a NC Wildlife Boat Ramp, observation area, and parking facilities to accommodate visiting fisherman, hunters and boaters. Community leaders continue to develop cultural heritage and eco-tourism initiatives that build on the area's natural resources.

Of course, like many small communities, Hamilton's most precious assets are the warm, generous, industrious people that make up the fabric of the community. It is these devoted community ambassadors that make Hamilton an exceptional place to live, work and visit.

Text - Carol Jones Shields
Above Right: Fort Branch Re-enactment. Photograph by Tony Kelly
Below Right: NC Wildlife Boat Access. Photograph by Carol Jones Shields

HAMILTON TOWNSHIP, FRANKLIN COUNTY, OHIO, 1807

Hamilton is one of the seventeen townships of Franklin County, Ohio. The 2010 census found 8,260 people, 4,438 of whom lived in the unincorporated portions of the township. It was organised under its present name in 1807.

HAMILTON SQUARE AND HAMILTON TOWNSHIP, MERCER COUNTY, NEW JERSEY, 1812

Hamilton Township is in Mercer County, New Jersey and has a population of around 89,000. The township is located immediately east of the city of Trenton, the capital of New Jersey. Located in central New Jersey, the township enjoys a prime location that is within an hour's drive of New York City, Philadelphia, and the Jersey Shore.

Covering nearly 40-square miles, it is very much a community of neighbourhoods – nestled with over 64 public parks and playgrounds that include Veterans Park, the beautiful Sayen Gardens, and acres of preserved open space. The residents enjoy numerous sports and recreational opportunities and come together throughout the year to celebrate special community events, such as at the annual Azalea Festival, Independence Day Fireworks and Concert celebration, SeptemberFest Community Day, Fall Harvest and Winter Wonderland.

Hamilton Township has a Civil War and Native American Museum that features Civil War exhibits and Delaware Indian artefacts.

Hamilton was incorporated as a township by an Act of the New Jersey Legislature on April 11, 1842, from portions of the now-defunct Nottingham Township. Hamilton Township derives its name from the village of Hamilton Square, which was named for Alexander Hamilton.

Although Hamilton is one of the largest townships in New Jersey it doesn't have a true "downtown", but a number of former "villages" form smaller commercial centres. These include Hamilton Square, Mercerville, Yardville, White Horse and Groveville.

Above: Sayen Gardens. Photograph by Daderot
Below: John Abbott House. Photograph by Blake Bollinger

Hamilton Square is a colonial village and suburban area which was founded in 1692. The Colonial Village is splendid and grand. Hamilton Square was named after Alexander Hamilton in a wave of anti-British feeling at the time of the War of 1812, having previously been called Nottingham after the English town.

There are a number of historical markers in Mercerville, many detailing the path of the Continental Army under the command of George Washington through the area during the American Revolutionary War, especially related to the night march from the Second Battle of Trenton to the Battle of Princeton.

Originally called "Sandtown," Mercerville is named after General Hugh Mercer who died on January 12, 1777 as a result of wounds incurred at the Battle of Princeton.

Isaac Watson House was built in 1708 on a bluff overlooking Watson's Creek.

John Abbott II House was built in 1730 by John Abbott and is located on the North side of Crosswicks Creek. The house is noted as being a secret repository for funds hidden from the British as they advanced on Trenton in 1776. The funds were stored by John Abbott II for State Treasurer Samuel Tucker inside a tub containing broken crockery. In 1969 the house was to be razed to the ground but was saved by the Hamilton Township Historical Society. The house is on the National Register.

Isaac Pearson House was built in 1733. Isaac Pearson was elected several times to the state assembly, served on the General Committee of Correspondence appointed by the Provincial Assembly July 21, 1774 and first Committee of Safety October 1775. In 1776, Isaac Pearson was murdered. Some accounts say he was murdered during a robbery; others say he was murdered for not fully supporting the cause of independence. The house is listed on the New Jersey Register of Historic Places.

Hamilton Township is a wonderful place to live, work, play and raise a family, and the township motto claims it to be "America's Favourite Hometown!"

Above Left: Fall at Gropp's Lake, Hamilton Township. Photograph by Frank R Bordentown
Below Left: Isaac Pearson House. Photograph by Blake Bollinger

HAMILTON, ATLANTIC COUNTY, NEW JERSEY, 1813

Hamilton was incorporated as a township by an Act of the New Jersey Legislature on February 5, 1813, from portions of Egg Harbor Township and Weymouth Township, while the area was still part of Gloucester County. Hamilton became part of the newly-created Atlantic County in 1837. Portions of the township were taken to form Hammonton on March 5, 1866, and to form Buena Vista Township on March 5, 1867.

Today Hamilton is a unique mix of two worlds: rural forest and bustling suburb. The western three-quarters of the township is rural pine forest protected from dense development by Pinelands Commission restrictions and large preserved tracts of land.

By stark contrast, the eastern quarter has developed as a suburban-like area due to its status as a Pinelands Regional Growth Area (RGA). Mandated to absorb growth

Above Left: County Courthouse. Photograph by Tim Kiser
Above: Mays Landing Presbyterian Church.
Photograph by Smallbones

fuelled by Atlantic City, Hamilton's RGA now is home to the majority of its 23,000 residents. It is also home to first class retail establishments including Hamilton Mall and Consumer Square.

The historic village of Mays Landing in Hamilton Township also has the distinction of being the County Seat of Atlantic County since 1837. Hamilton is also home to the Atlantic County Institute of Technology, the Atlantic County Justice Facility, and the County Court Complex.

Hamilton Township's origins are directly tied to the Great Egg Harbor River and its tributaries which run through it. George May, after whom the village of Mays Landing was named, built a shipyard and trading post near Babcock Creek in 1756. By the mid - 19th century Mays Landing had reached the height of its shipbuilding years.

From 1830 to 1880, more than two hundred vessels were built along the Great Egg Harbor River, with lumber from native forests and iron from Weymouth foundries. Half of them were produced at Mays Landing, but by the end of century, wood shipbuilding began to disappear due to the lack of suitable timber. Iron was then substituted for hull construction.

Today, the Great Egg Harbor River and Lake Lenape are recreational resources used by local residents and visitors alike. In the new millennium Hamilton has continued to grow, offering a modern community with all the amenities of suburban life while preserving the peaceful lifestyle of a rural community and the rich history of Mays Landing Village.

The Great Egg Harbor River is a 55 mile-long river in southern New Jersey in the United States. It is one of the major rivers that traverse the largely pristine Pinelands, draining 308 square miles of wetlands into the Atlantic Ocean at Great Egg Harbor, from which it takes its name.

Great Egg Harbor (and thus the river) got its name from Dutch explorer Cornelius Jacobsen Mey. In 1614, Mey came upon the inlet to the Great Egg Harbor River. The meadows were so covered with shorebird and waterfowl eggs that he called it "Eyren Haven" (Egg Harbor). Today, the National Park Service considers it one of the top 10 places in North America for birding.

Great Egg Harbor River. Photograph by Bill Wright

Mays Landing. Photograph by Tim Kiser

HAMILTON, MADISON COUNTY, NEW YORK STATE, 1816

Hamilton, New York, home of Colgate University, is a village of approximately 3,700, which swells to 6,500 when Colgate is in session. It is located in the Town of Hamilton, Madison County, and is close to the geographic centre of New York State. The Village encompasses approximately 2.5 square miles, while the Town, with a population of 2,200 not counting the village, covers about 41.4 square miles and is largely rural; its main "industry" being dairy farming. Increasing numbers of Amish people are buying land that has been abandoned by other farmers in the Town, and dramatically enriching the land, building barns, and improving the farmsteads. They are very hard-working, law-abiding folk, and the efforts of their labours are one of the main attractions at the village's Farmers' Market. It is still somewhat unusual, but pleasing, to see the Amish in their horse drawn buggies on the Town and Village roads.

The land where Hamilton now stands once belonged to the Oneida and Stockbridge Indians, tribes of the Iroquois Nation. A treaty was signed in 1788 which allowed the land to be purchased by New York State. In 1794 a wealthy New York merchant, who owned many acres in the region, sold the land that is now Hamilton and Colgate to Samuel Payne and his wife. In the next year, they were joined by Samuel's brother Elisha, and several other families. The "village" was first named "Payne's Settlement" in 1795. The two brothers were later to become among the 13 men who founded what is now Colgate University. By 1800, "Payne's Settlement" had more than 25 houses. The first public building was a log schoolhouse, built sometime before 1800. A frame building took its place in 1800, and was used for public meetings and church services as well as for a school.

In 1816, "Payne's Settlement" received a charter from the State of New York and was incorporated as a village named Hamilton, after Alexander Hamilton, George Washington's Secretary of the Treasury, who was greatly admired by Elisha Payne. Payne became Hamilton's first President.

Hamilton is now governed by an elected Mayor and four elected Trustees, with an annual budget of approximately $7 million. Although considered a village, Hamilton is much like a small city, possessing not only a small university, but also a community hospital, the county's only airport, its own Municipal Utilities Corporation, a police department,

Village Lit Up For Christmas. Photograph by Robert Cornell

a volunteer fire department, and a mostly volunteer emergency ambulance corps.

There is one school, serving kindergarten through to 12th grade students, and the youngsters from surrounding hamlets and villages are bussed to it each day. Hamilton has five churches, a Post Office, and a public library which is the focus of much of the village's activity. A newspaper, the Mid-York Weekly, is published once a week, and there has been a newspaper, under various names, in Hamilton since the early 1800's.

Village Square in Summer

Relations between the Village and Colgate are very good. The Hamilton Initiative, was formed about 10 years ago, consisting of representatives from both Colgate and the Village serving on its Board, originally to beautify the downtown storefronts. Thanks to the Hamilton Initiative, Hamilton enjoys a movie theatre which shows a wide array of offerings; the Palace Theatre, where live plays and musical events are performed; many and varied restaurants; and the Colgate Bookstore which is located in the heart of the village, making it easily accessible to townspeople. An attractive village green runs through the centre of the downtown and is the location of a thriving farmers' market from May to early November.

Colgate's campus and most of its buildings are located on a hill, a short walk from the Village. Many of the buildings are built from stone, taken from a quarry adjacent to the campus. For many years, people have referred to "on the hill" when speaking of Colgate. It was founded in 1819 by thirteen very religious Baptists who were concerned that there were very few Baptist ministers to serve the growing area of Central New York. Colgate's original purpose was as a seminary to train Baptist ministers. It was named The Baptist Educational Society, and later became Madison University. It was not until 1890 that it became Colgate University, in honour of the generous donations of the Colgate family. Colgate no longer has any connection with the Baptist faith, and ranks among the top small liberal arts colleges in the United States. Hamiltonians are very lucky in that most of Colgate's facilities are open to townspeople, many of them free of charge.

Although small, Hamilton is a great place to live! Besides its many advantages, already mentioned, it is situated in a lovely part of New York State. Hamilton is located in the Chenango Valley, with many evidences of glacial terrain in its geography. It is surrounded by rolling countryside, hills, ponds and lakes. It enjoys four distinct seasons of the year – warm, but not uncomfortably hot, summers; Fall, marked by the turning of many of the leaves to beautiful orange, yellow, and red; generally very cold and snowy winters; and finally, Spring, when the leaves pop out and many kinds of flowers start to bloom. The people are friendly and there is genuine community spirit throughout. Colgate's students add a lively atmosphere to the village that many small towns lack.

The Hamilton Rotary Club thrives in the village!

Text – Debbie Kliman

Above: Colgate University Campus and the Town
Below: The Colgate Inn where Rotary meets
All unattributed Photographs by John Hubbard

Sunset over Hamilton

Taylor Lake at Colgate University. Photograph by Margie Bikovsky

Long Pond in the Adirondack Park

Raquette Lake Village in Hamilton County

HAMILTON COUNTY, NEW YORK, 1816

Hamilton County is located in the state of New York, and is quite distinct from the town described previously. It is named after Alexander Hamilton, the only member of the New York State delegation who signed the United States Constitution in 1787, and later became the first United States Secretary of the Treasury. Its county seat is Lake Pleasant. It is one of only two counties that lie entirely within the Adirondack Park (Essex being the other). It is the least populous of New York's 62 counties and also the most sparsely populated county in the eastern half of the United States, with a population density of just over 3 people per square mile. Curiously there is no permanent traffic light in the whole of Hamilton County.

In 1816, Hamilton County was created by partitioning 1,800 square miles from Montgomery County, but due to low population it remained unorganized and was administered from Montgomery County, until it was recognized as sufficiently organized for self-government in 1838. The organization process was completed by summer of 1847.

In 1860, Fulton County was partitioned, with 10 square miles of land in Sacandaga Park transferred to Hamilton County.

In 1915, land was swapped between Hamilton and Essex counties, with Hamilton ceding Fishing Brook Mountain for Indian Lake. Hamilton gained an additional 20 square miles, whereas Essex County lost 30 square miles. This left Hamilton with its present size of 1,830 square miles.

The former town of Gilman was dissolved in 1860. The original county seat was Sageville, now part of Lake Pleasant.

HAMILTON TOWNSHIP, WARREN COUNTY, OHIO, 1818

Hamilton Township, Warren County is located in the south west corner of the great State of Ohio. In the shape of a rectangle, Hamilton Township is approximately six and a half miles from north to south, and approximately five and a half miles from east to west, comprising an area of thirty four square miles. The township is bounded on the north and west by the Little Miami State and National Scenic River and on the south by Clermont County, Ohio.

Hamilton Township was ranked as one of the top ten, Tri-State Area Communities in 2009 and is still the fastest growing community in Warren County. The 2010 United States Census estimates 23,556 residents within the community, more than doubling the population since the 2000 Census.

This quiet, dormitory community boasts two country clubs, golf courses, a vineyard and canoeing on the Little Miami River.

Hamilton Township is named for Alexander Hamilton, one of the Founding Fathers and the first United States Secretary of Treasury. Hamilton Township is one of the original four townships created when Warren County was divided in May, 1803. By June, 1818, the boundaries of the township were permanently established.

One of the major north-south trails used by Native American people once ran through Hamilton Township, with evidence still discernible on lands near Zoar. Stone implements and weapons of the native Neolithic and Paleolithic "Mound Builders" can still be found throughout the township.

The township's first continuously inhabited town, Hopkinsville, dates back to 1808. Other villages in Hamilton Township include Zoar, established at an early time, but the year is not known for certain. Murdoch, situated on what was known as Murdoch Pike, was named for Dr.James E. Murdoch who made his home there. Cozaddale was laid out by John J. Cozad in 1871. Cozad's house, built in 1843, is still standing today and is located on Murdoch-Cozaddale Road. Organized in 1878 by Joseph Warren King, the Kings Powder and Peters Cartridge Companies is located on some 500 acres of land along the Little Miami River. The cartridge company was built in 1887 to produce loaded shells for the black powder manufactured by King Powder.

Canoeing on the Little Miami River

Peters Cartridge Company was sold to Remington Arms in 1934. The companies specialized in ammunitions production throughout the American Civil War, World War I and World War II. The landmark shot tower, used in the manufacturing of lead pellets, still stands and its likeness is now an important component of Hamilton Township's logo.

Hamilton Township strives to draw from its history as it progresses forward into the future. Hamilton Township operates as a grassroot form of "Home Rule" Limited Self-Government with a strong political leadership of three Trustees and a Fiscal Officer, each of whom are elected to a four year term.

Hamilton Township Administration Building

Hamilton Township provides twenty-four hour coverage with full-time professional staff from the Police, Fire and Road departments. In addition over ninety miles of roadway, three township cemeteries and two private cemeteries are maintained within the jurisdiction. Hamilton Township oversees nearly 800 acres of township-owned park land. The four largest parks (Testerman, Nunner, Mounts and Marr) offer baseball diamonds, tennis courts, basketball courts, football and soccer fields, concessions, and horseshoe pits. There is a special enclosed area for toddlers and a picnic area that includes four shelters, barbecue pits and picnic tables. A recent addition to the parks in this township is Big Foot Run Dog Park which is situated on seven acres of Ancient American Native preservation land.

The Peters Cartridge Factory

Winding through Hamilton Township along the Little Miami Scenic River is 13.5 miles of the Little Miami Bike Trail. The entire bike trail is more than 100 miles long and is the longest paved trail in the United States. Hamilton Township is strategically located within the Cincinnati area and is a host to several recreational events. With Warren County known as "Ohio's Largest Playground", residents and visitors look forward to the Berry Festival, TPA golf conference, and events for all ages throughout the year.

The annual Berry Festival provides a wondrous summer weekend filled with family, neighbours and friends meeting at the park to enjoy live entertainment and a finale showcasing magnificent fireworks.

Battle of Chattanooga

HAMILTON COUNTY, TENNESSEE, 1819

Hamilton County is located in the state of Tennessee. The population is over 300,000 and its county seat is Chattanooga.

Hamilton County was formed on October 25, 1819 from portions of Rhea County and Native American Indian land. It was named after Alexander Hamilton, an officer in the American Revolutionary War, member of Continental Congress, first US Secretary of Treasury, and one of the Founding Fathers of the United States.

The first settlers were Scotsmen, who located here very soon after the Revolution. Among the names preserved are Ross, McNair, McCoy, Coody, Martin, Taylor, Adair, Lourie, McPherson and McDonald. Most of these men married Native Americans, and became incorporated into the Cherokee Nation. John Ross became a chief of the Cherokees. At the time the county was organized the population was 821, of whom 766 were of European descent.

Battlefield Museum in the Fall

The present site of Chattanooga was formerly Ross's Landing. It took its name from the Scotsman, Ross, or his descendants, but did not come to prominence until the place began to become a salt market for the salt works far up the Tennessee River in Virginia.

In 1836 the military post was established here. This new tract of land became known as the Ocoee District, and the land office was at Cleveland. Pre-emption rights were given to all those who had already made improvements. The town was named Chattanooga upon being laid out, but the meaning of the name is uncertain, though the origin is doubtless from the Native American Indians. In 1839 the town was incorporated as such, and in 1851 was chartered as a city. In the thirties the project of uniting Cincinnati and Charleston, South Carolina, with a railroad was discussed. This finally brought a road from the south to Chattanooga in 1849. At this time the city was a brisk commercial port, and was steadily growing.

Hamilton County was the site of an important saltpetre mine during the American Civil War. Saltpetre is the main ingredient of gunpowder and was obtained by leaching the earth from caves. Lookout Mountain Cave was a major source of saltpetre during the American Civil War. The mine was operated by Robert Cravens, who owned the property where the cave is located. In May 1861, Cravens contracted with the Tennessee Military and Financial Board to deliver 20,000 pounds of saltpetre. On the 24th of the same month, he reported that he had ten hoppers already set up in his cave. Cravens was also mining Nickajack Cave in nearby Marion County. In 1862 he quit mining at Lookout Mountain Cave and rented it to the Confederate Nitre Bureau, which mined the cave from June 1862 through July 1863. Mining ceased when Chattanooga was occupied by Federal forces in 1863.

After the Civil War, the governments of Chattanooga and Tennessee were both nearly bankrupt, but in July, 1866, Tennessee became the first Confederate state to be readmitted to the Union. Since further military occupation seemed unlikely the way seemed clear for Chattanooga to get back on the track toward growth. Essentially, this path involved the same activities which had driven pre-war Chattanooga: attracting

Above: Chattanooga Choo Choo. Photograph by Matt Girling
Below: Revitalised Waterfront

Walnut Street Bridge

Terminal Station: Home to The Chattanooga Choo Choo.
Photograph by Matt Girling

industry and exploiting to the fullest the already existent possibilities of river and rail transportation.

As the 20th Century moved forward, Chattanooga's riverfront underwent massive changes. Higher water levels along the Tennessee River allowed many companies on or near the river to operate their own wharfs. Steam engines lost out to diesel-powered engines early in the century, and these powerful boats were (and continue to be) used to tow large barges filled with grain, salt, sand, coal, lime or gravel. The long-time competitor of river transport, the railroads, also ceased to hold as much importance as automotive modes of transport worked their way into American culture. An elaborate and far-reaching highway and interstate system made travel and transport by road the primary source of transportation in America by the middle of the century, and increasing traffic in the Chattanooga area led to dramatic changes on the riverfront.

By the 1930s Chattanooga was known as the "Dynamo of Dixie", inspiring the 1941 Glenn Miller big-band swing song "Chattanooga Choo Choo". However, the same mountains that provided Chattanooga's scenic backdrop also served to trap industrial pollutants which caused them to settle over the community; so much so that in 1969, the federal government declared that Chattanooga's air was the dirtiest in the nation. Environmental crises were not the only problems plaguing the city. Like other early industrial cities, Chattanooga entered the 1980s with serious socioeconomic challenges, including job layoffs due to de-industrialization, a deteriorating city infrastructure, racial tensions and social division. Due to these factors, Chattanooga's population declined by more than 10% in the 1980s.

View of City at Night from Point Park

Chattanooga Incline Railway   *Icarus Statue*

In recent years, private and governmental resources have been invested in transforming the city's tarnished image. They have worked to revitalize its downtown and riverfront areas, making use of its natural resources. An early cornerstone of this project was the restoration of the historic Walnut Street Bridge, which is the oldest surviving bridge of its kind in the Southeastern United States.

The "21st Century Waterfront Plan", a $120 million redevelopment of the Chattanooga waterfront and downtown area, was completed in 2005. The Tennessee Aquarium, which opened in 1992, has become a major waterfront attraction that has helped to spur neighbourhood development. Chattanooga has garnered numerous accolades for the transformation of its image.

Photographs provided by Chattanooga Area Convention and Visitors Bureau

Above: Bluff View Art District and Hunter Museum
Below: Coolidge Park

Tennessee River in the Fall. Photograph provided by Warren McClelland Photography

HAMILTON COUNTY, ILLINOIS, 1821

McCoy Memorial Library and Bank. Photograph by Kathy Teffertiller

St James Episcopal Church. Photograph by Mallory Minor

In the spring of 1821 the Illinois Legislature appointed three men to select a location for the county seat in Hamilton County, which was named after Revolutionary War Hero and the first United States Secretary of Treasury, Alexander Hamilton. Hamilton County had been struck off from White County only a few years earlier. The place was selected from a little 20 acre farm that belonged to Dr William McLean who lived in the centre of what is today known as the public square. The gentlemen only saw it fitting to name the city in honour of the man who so graciously sold them the land, and so the city was named McLeansboro.

Before there was a courthouse all business that was held in the county was conducted at John Anderson's home. One of the first transactions of business was to build a court house. It was a little house built of wood logs and had one window. The price to build this little one room court house was $379 and it was constructed by Mr Benjamin Hood.

The first school to be built in the county was voted on in the fall of 1877. It cost a little over $9,000. It was made of brick and had fencing, grounds, and a coal house. The first principal was Mr Leonidas Walker. The first church to be built in the county, built at a cost of $1200 in 1843, belonged to the congregation of the Methodist denomination.

As of the 2010 census there are a total of 8,457, residents living within a total area of 435.89 square miles. The county has three main highways that run through it with Interstate 64 on its northern boundary, and is comprised of six different towns: Belle Prairie City, Broughton, Dahlgren, Dale, Macedonia, and the largest being McLeansboro. The entire county is made up of twelve townships, which are all represented in the County Board. The coldest month is January which has an average temperature of 20 degrees Fahrenheit, and the warmest month is July and has an average temperature of 89 degrees Fahrenheit.

A Combine Harvester in the fields of Hamilton County.
Photograph by Marty Cox

Hamilton County is primarily an agricultural community with corn, soybeans and wheat as the main crops; with some cattle and swine operations scattered throughout the county. Currently, a new coal mine is under construction in the northwest quarter of the county with potential for additional mines to be constructed in the future. The local hospital just underwent an 18.5 million dollar renovation and additions project. The school district is a county district and houses a preschool, two elementary schools and a modern Junior-Senior High School.

The county has four buildings in the National Register of Historical Listings. They are: The Cloud State Bank, which is still in use today as a part of Peoples National Bank; The Aaron G. Cloud House, which is the County's Public Library and home of the Hamilton County Historical Society Museum and Genealogy; The Chalon Guard and Emma Blades Cloud House; and the St James Episcopal Church.

Hamilton County Courthouse. Photograph by Kathy Teffertiller

The little county is strong but mighty, and all have a great sense of pride in the little community of Hamilton County. Community service is a strong component of the benefits of living in the county with the Rotary Club just having celebrated its 25th anniversary with a membership of 32 members.

Dolan Lake in Hamilton County, Illinois. Photograph by Kathy Teffertiller

HAMILTON COUNTY, INDIANA, 1823

Hamilton County, Indiana, is a northern suburb of Indianapolis, Indiana. It is one of several counties that comprise the "donut", so called because they form a geographic ring around the city of Indianapolis.

The land containing Hamilton County was brought into the possession of the United States by the Treaty of St. Mary's in 1818. William Conner was the first European settler in the county. In the summer of 1822, after realizing there were enough settlers in the area, Conner and other settlers applied to the Indiana Legislature for a charter authorizing them to become a separate and independent county under Indiana law. The application was presented to the Legislature at the 1822-23 session and the act was passed and approved by the governor on January 8, 1823. The act took effect on the first Monday in April 1823. The County Commissioners first met on May 5, 1823, at the house of William Conner. Conner's house would also serve as the County Circuit Court. The county was named after Alexander Hamilton, the First Secretary of the Treasury.

Politically, it is one of the most conservative counties in the nation.

Hamilton County was largely rural until about 30 years ago, when high speed highways and inexpensive land made suburban living very attractive. Hamilton County became the suburban community of choice for many Indianapolis residents and the population has been growing ever since.

Above Left: The 19th century courthouse was restored in the 1990's and is still used today. Photograph by Derek Jensen

Below Left: The Village of West Clay is a new urbanism style development. Photograph by Derek Jensen

Today, it is one of the fastest-growing counties in the United States and the fastest growing in Indiana. The county's population jumped from an estimated 182,740 in 2000 to 261,661 in 2007, and measures more than 300,000 today. The growth proceeded through the economic recession and is expected to continue. It is now the fourth most populous county in Indiana.

The communities are attractive largely due to the quality of their schools. There is a highly educated population. More than half of adults hold a college degree, and they are willing to spend public money on education, recognizing that good schools attract people and business. Ironically, there is no higher education institution based in Hamilton County, though there are several satellite campuses located there.

There are eight cities and towns in Hamilton County. Along the southern border, Carmel and Fishers vie for the title of most populous city (though Fishers is technically a town instead of a city, meaning it is governed by a town board and manager instead of a mayor). Noblesville is the seat of county government and is well-known for its historic second-empire-style county courthouse and surrounding square. It is a rare example of a thriving historic downtown in a state where many downtowns struggle to survive against competition from national chain stores. People enjoy the quaint character of the historic buildings.

Westfield is the newest city, having switched from a town just a few years ago. It has big plans to become the family sports capital of the U.S. and is investing millions of dollars in a sports campus to attract that business. US31, a primary north-south state highway, is currently undergoing a major upgrade and Westfield is planning to rebuild its downtown as the highway is completed.

Above Right: Downtown Carmel is designated as its Arts and Design District, featuring locally owned art galleries and the Indiana Design Centre as well as restaurants and boutiques. Photograph by Mike Corbett

Below Right: Morse Lake Cicero: One of two lakes in Hamilton County that offer year round lakeside living

Four smaller towns: Cicero, Arcadia, Atlanta and Sheridan, are all in various stages of renovation. All were once served by the railroads and used to be larger than they are now. As the railroads declined, so did these towns. There are currently no railroads operating in Hamilton County but the small towns are thriving as they serve new residents who enjoy small town living.

Carmel has enjoyed some well-deserved attention recently for transforming a sleepy downtown into a thriving suburb with a robust arts community. An Arts and Design District defines Main St. and features a varied selection of art galleries and locally-owned restaurants. A short walk away by trail is a performing arts complex anchored by a brand new concert hall called the Palladium, which is fast earning a reputation as one of the most acoustically perfect performance spaces in the nation.

Carmel is also the roundabout capital of the U.S., featuring about 75 of the signature traffic intersections, more than any other city in the U.S.. Urged on by an ambitious mayor, Carmel continues to build them, claiming they save money, time and lives. Other communities around the U.S. and Hamilton County are taking notice and building their own, but the trend started in Carmel, which also claims the distinction of erecting the first traffic signal more than 100 years ago.

Above Left: Raiders Entering Dupont: Conner Prairie's 1863 Civil War Journey exhibition recreates a raid on tiny Dupont, Indiana, by a Confederate raiding party, the only Civil War battle fought in Indiana.

Below Left: Roundabout at 106th and Keystone: Carmel is the roundabout capital of the nation

The county has a robust interest in history, as exemplified by the main tourist attraction, Conner Prairie. Located in Fishers, Conner Prairie is one of the finest living history parks in the nation. It is located on land donated by Eli Lilly of Lilly Pharmaceuticals, Indianapolis's most generous philanthropist. It is a destination for thousands of schoolchildren throughout the region, who can interact with people who portray historical figures, to learn about life on the prairie in the 1800's. It is named for William Conner, the first white settler in the county, whose original homestead was on this land.

The welcome mat is out in Hamilton County. Although growth has been prodigious, communities remain open to new people and new businesses as the County continues to set a high standard for suburban living in Central Indiana and the Midwest.

Text- Mike Corbett

Hamilton Town Centre: A brand new regional outdoor mall finished recently in Noblesville. Photograph by Mike Corbett

There is an abundance of older, traditional style homes. Photograph by Mike Corbett

Palladium and Carmel City Centre: The Palladium is an acoustically perfect performance hall opened in 2011 and is drawing world class performers.

FORT HAMILTON ARMY BASE, BROOKLYN, NEW YORK, 1825

Historic Fort Hamilton is located in the south-western corner of the New York City borough of Brooklyn.

On July 4, 1776, a small American battery on the site of today's Fort Hamilton (the east side of the Narrows) fired into one of the British men-of-war convoying troops to suppress the American Revolution. HMS Asia suffered damage and casualties, but opposition to the immense fleet could be little more than symbolic. The very significant event, however, marked one of the earliest uses of the site for military purposes.

The War of 1812 underscored the importance of coastal defence and helped to promote a new round of fort building. The cornerstone for Fort Hamilton was set in place on June 11, 1825. Six years and half a million dollars later, the fort was ready to receive its garrison.

Though references to the structure as Fort Hamilton occur as early as 1826, it was not officially named for the former Senior Officer of the United States Army and first Secretary of the Treasury, Alexander Hamilton, until the twentieth century. In 1839 the Federal Government gave permission to New York State's 27th Regiment to drill at the fort, thus qualifying it as the nation's first National Guard training camp. The following year it allocated $20,000 to improve the fort's armaments, and Captain Robert E. Lee was assigned the task of improving its defences, as well as those of other military installations in the area. Lee served as Fort Hamilton's post engineer from 1841 to 1846. Lieutenant Thomas "Stonewall" Jackson also served at Fort Hamilton.

During the Civil War, Fort Hamilton's garrison expanded. A ship barrier across the Narrows assisted Fort Hamilton and its sister fort on Staten Island, now called Fort Wadsworth, in protecting the harbour against the possibility of Confederate raiders. The forts also provided troops to help put down the New York Draft Riots of 1863. Rifled cannon made vertical-walled masonry fortifications obsolete during the American Civil War, and in the last decades of the nineteenth century great advances in military technology brought a whole new generation of long-range guns mounted in inconspicuous emplacements. In the two World Wars, Fort Hamilton served as a major embarkation and separation centre.

Entrance to Army Base at Fort Hamilton

St John's Episcopal Church. The Garrison Church. Outside the Fort's gates

At present the United States Army Fort Hamilton Garrison is the home of the New York City Recruiting Battalion, the Military Entrance Processing Station, the North Atlantic Division Headquarters of the United States Army Corps of Engineers, the 1179th Transportation Brigade and the 722nd Aeromedical Staging Squadron. Fort Hamilton also supports many Reserve and National Guard units.

The original fort later became the Officer's Club and now houses the Community Club. The caponier (a miniature fort guarding the main fort's gate) now houses the Harbour Defence Museum. Other notable landmarks include the Robert E. Lee House, where Lee (then a captain) resided while commander of the garrison, and Colonel's Row, six historic townhouses used to house senior officers. All of these structures are listed on the National Register of Historic Places.

This century the historic parade field (that once lay behind the old New York Area Command (NYAC) Headquarters Building and the Military Personnel Office), former site of numerous ceremonies and festivities, was developed into swiftly built privatized housing. The historic flag pole and cannon are still present at the site, near the old headquarters building.

The entrance to the Defence Museum at Fort Hamilton

Cannons at Fort Hamilton which used to defend New York Harbour. Photographs supplied by millefiorifavoriti.blogspot.com

HAMILTON COUNTY, FLORIDA, 1827

Hamilton County is located in the U.S. state of Florida and has a population of about 14,000 with Jasper as its county seat.

Hamilton County was created in 1827 from portions of Jefferson County. It was named after Alexander Hamilton, First Secretary of the Treasury. Hamilton County is a rural area, rich in history, and loaded with real Southern charm. One of the largest industries is phosphate mining.

There were many men in the county that chose to fight in battles in the American Civil War, 1861-1865, leaving their families at home to earn a meagre living from the local farms. Crops were slim, as there was a shortage of male labour to help tend them. The County Commissioners bought and provided corn, salt, and other supplies to those needy families that could not fend for themselves.

Johns House in the White Springs Historic District

Adams House in the White Springs Historic District

Alapaha River

United Methodist Church, Jasper

Men from the county joined many units of the Confederate Army, and then there were those who did not believe in the Confederate causes and consequently joined the Union Army. Some men willingly volunteered to serve in the Army; others were forced because of a law that was passed ordering all men aged 18 to 45 to serve. Although some men could pay other men to serve in their places, most of those from Hamilton County were unable to do so, and therefore, had to fight themselves.

Hamilton County is located in North Central Florida, with Georgia forming its northern border. The county (often called a peninsula within a peninsula) is separated from the rest of Florida by the Withlacoochee River on the west and the beautiful Suwannee River to the east and south. In the middle of the county is the fascinating Alapaha River, called the "River of Sand," which disappears underground during certain parts of the year leaving a dry, sandy river bed.

There are a number of historic buildings including the United Methodist Church and the Old Jail in Jasper.

The White Springs Historic District encompasses approximately 1,200 acres, and contains 81 historic buildings.

All Photographs supplied by Ebyabe

HAMILTON, GEORGIA, 1828

Hamilton, Georgia is located in the South Eastern United States of America on the West Central side of Harris County. It is located 75 miles southwest of Atlanta, Georgia, which is the state capital and largest city. Hamilton is conveniently only 20 miles north of Columbus, Georgia, the third largest city in the state, which borders the boundary of Fort Benning United States Army Post. The Chattahoochee River borders the west side of Harris County. The town is considered to be in the foothills at the southernmost tip of the Appalachian Mountains. Hamilton is in close proximity to the Interstate network which makes it easy to travel to work, airports, shopping, restaurants, and sporting or cultural events in Columbus, LaGrange, and Atlanta.

Hamilton, the county seat, was incorporated in 1828. Prior to that date the area was part of the Creek Indian Springs holdings until the Treaty of Indian Springs in 1825. The first white settlers arrived soon after the Native American Indians were forced to leave, as part of the treaty agreement, and land lots were offered through state lotteries to settlers from Pennsylvania, Virginia, the Carolinas, and, of course, to Georgians.

Harris County Courthouse, Hamilton. Photograph by Rivers Langley

The Old Jail. Jasper

The Little White House

The city of Hamilton is believed to be named for James Hamilton, Jr., a governor of South Carolina. Mr Hamilton is known for passing the Nullification Ordinance in 1832 and for leading the armed forces to defend the state's rights. The county was named in memory of Charles Harris, a beloved lawyer and mayor of Savannah, Georgia. Mr Harris was the son-in-law of a Revolutionary War patriot.

The lovely city is governed by elected officials: a mayor and four city councillors and the population is just over a thousand. The Harris County School System is accredited by the Southern Association of Colleges and Schools and considered to be one of the best in the state. Hamilton is home to an active Harris County Chamber of Commerce which hosts the annual Wheels On Fire Cycle Tour, a Century Cycle Tour that attracts cyclists from throughout the United States. Hamilton is six miles south of Callaway Gardens, a family vacation resort in Pine Mountain, Georgia, set on 14,000 acres of natural beauty with a man-made beach, lakes, fishing, golf, tennis, and bike/hiking trails. Callaway Gardens showcases native plants, flowers, and birds while providing popular events like Fantasy in Lights and the Masters Water Ski and

Civil War Monument in Hamilton. Photograph by Rivers Langley

Wakeboard Tournament and plenty of accommodation. About two miles east of downtown Hamilton, the Harris County Cattleman's Association sponsors their annual professional rodeo, a popular event in beautiful Pine Mountain Valley. Hundreds of visitors also attend the Ossahatchee Indian Festival and Pow-Wow each fall in the same location. Other areas of interest include Pine Mountain, Franklin D. Roosevelt State Park, Warm Springs, and the Little White House, former President Roosevelt's home and museum.

Hamilton is a great place to live with a lovely rural setting, large open spaces with creeks and lakes. This gives campers, hunters, and fishermen ample opportunities to enjoy their hobbies and fill the freezer with bream, bass, turkey, dove, and venison. The city is a "step-back-in-time" with friendly residents, a walking trail near City Hall, and a beautiful town square. Across the street is the court house dating to 1908 (with an annex completed in 1998). Visitors enjoy photographing its Neoclassical Revival style and our quaint downtown area. Y'all come see us!

Text and unattributed Photographs supplied by Becky Chambers, Mayor of Hamilton

JAMES HAMILTON JR. (1786 – 1857)

James Hamilton, Jr. was an American lawyer and politician. He represented South Carolina in the U.S. Congress (1822–1829) and served as its 53rd Governor (1830–1832).

James was born on May 8, 1786 in Charleston, South Carolina to James Hamilton and Elizabeth Lynch, daughter of Congressman Thomas Lynch and sister of Thomas Lynch, Jr. He practised law in Charleston, and for several years served the city as its mayor. He was elected to the South Carolina state House of Representatives, and served from 1819 until 1822. When William Lowndes resigned from the U.S. Congress, Hamilton was elected to complete his term, and started his congressional career on December 13, 1822. He was re-elected in 1824 and 1826. He was a States' Rights Democrat and a Nullifier.

Hamilton personally loaned $216,000 to the young Republic of Texas, and arranged other loans for them from the Bank of the United States. He served as a special agent for them in Europe, gaining diplomatic recognition for the new republic from Great Britain and Holland. He finally moved to Texas in 1855.

In 1857, while returning to Texas from Washington, D.C., Hamilton's steam-boat was sunk, and he drowned in the Gulf of Mexico, reportedly after yielding his seat in a lifeboat to a woman and her child.

HAMILTON, CLINTON COUNTY, INDIANA, 1830

Hamilton is an unincorporated community in Madison Township, Clinton County, Indiana. The town is named for Alexander Hamilton.

The western portion of the land on which Hamilton stands was settled by Jacob Stetler in late 1829 or 1830, and the eastern part by John Gallinger in 1831, the two being separated by what is now Hamilton Road. According to a 1913 history of Clinton County, "tradition has it that these two men met under the shade of a tree, near where the two highways cross, on a Sunday and agreed to join in laying out the town plat, which agreement was thereafter carried to execution..." The plat included 36 lots each on the east and west sides of the road.

The first house in Hamilton was built by John Jamison, a saddler, who also ran a small shop.

Hamilton reached a population of more than a hundred and was an active business centre for the community, but it was eclipsed by nearby Mulberry which had the only railroad station in the township, and gradually dwindled during the late 19th and early 20th centuries. It now consists of about a dozen homes.

Aerial View of Hamilton Lake, Hamilton, Steuben County.
Photograph by Eyster Photo

FORT HAMILTON, WISCONSIN, 1832

Fort Hamilton was one of the hastily constructed frontier forts built in Wisconsin with the onset of the 1832 Black Hawk War. Fort Hamilton was located in present-day Wiota, Wisconsin (then Hamilton's Diggings) near the location of the modern settlement. During the course of the Black Hawk War no attack was made on Fort Hamilton but four members of its garrison were killed during the war. The stockade was a 40 foot by 40 foot square with a 16 foot by 24 foot blockhouse and was surrounded by a ditch and pickets.

HAMILTON, STEUBEN COUNTY, INDIANA, 1838

In the late 1830s, the land that present-day Hamilton was built on was sold by the owner Niconar Munson to Dr Samuel Tuttle, who was the first to plat the town. The original name of the town was "Enterprise". Dr Tuttle went to New York shortly thereafter, where he met Fisher Howe, president of a syndicate of capitalists. Dr Tuttle sold all but one-sixteenth of the plat to him for $15,000.

In the spring of 1838, Howe sent Sidney Gambia, an agent, to Enterprise to sell goods and develop the settlement. However, Enterprise was greatly affected by illness that year, to such an extent that it became known for it. To improve the settlement's reputation, the name was changed to Hamilton.

Eventually the town was sold to Sidney Gambia for $1 (and for other terms), and the name was officially recorded as the Town of Hamilton in 1844.

Although it has always remained a small town, historically the population explodes in the summer months due to the appeal of the wonderful lake.

Hamilton Lake covers over 800 acres with a depth of over 90 feet. Downtown Hamilton is located along the south shore of the lake, offering many restaurants, merchants and professional services.

Left: Lake Views. Photographs by Den Albertson
Text - Milton Otero - Clerk, Town of Hamilton

NEWTON HAMILTON, MIFFLIN COUNTY, PENNSYLVANIA, 1843

Newton Hamilton was incorporated in 1843. A settler named Hugh Brown originally lived on the land in 1762. He was killed by Native American Indians and his half-sisters, named Hamilton, inherited the land. The Pennsylvania Canal also contributed to the growth of Newton Hamilton. It is named after the town of Newtonhamilton in County Armagh, Northern Ireland. The population is now around 200.

HAMILTON, BOONE COUNTY, KENTUCKY, 1846

Hamilton is an unincorporated town in Boone County, Kentucky. It is situated in the southern part of the county on the Ohio River; it is about a mile north of the mouth of Big Bone Creek. It was established in 1835, being incorporated by the Kentucky Legislature as the Town of Landing. The plat was laid out by Joel Hamilton and George McGlasson.

In 1846 the name of the town was changed to Hamilton in honour of Joel Hamilton, the founder, who had since moved to Texas. The town was authorized to levy taxes the next year. This was a real estate tax, not to exceed fifty cents per hundred dollars.

The limits of the town of Hamilton were extended in 1849. A provision was added by the legislature that citizens of the town were not required to work on the road more than half a mile beyond the new limit. In 1852 a new road, the Hamilton and Union Turnpike, was chartered. This may have been in conjunction with the incorporation of the Big Bone Hotel Company at the nearby Big Bone Springs the previous year. Other projects chartered in the area that year were the Napoleon and Big Bone Lick Turnpike, and the Union and Beaver Turnpike.

This seems to have been the high point of the town's history, though it was still a community up into the early part of the twentieth century. Hamilton was a busy town in the nineteenth century, with a mill, two tobacco warehouses, two doctors, a general store, a school and possibly a distillery. Lewis Loder, a magistrate and tavern keeper from Petersburg, Kentucky, in the same county, records going downriver to Hamilton on the steamer to purchase barrels of Whiskey. In 1883, the Garnett, Johnson, Black, Story and Davis families lived and worked along the river in Hamilton. Dr John A. Wood advertised a specialization in chronic cases where he practised at Big Bone Springs.

Hamilton is the last town along the Ohio River in Boone County. The town was likely settled in the early nineteenth century due to its proximity to Big Bone Springs and Big Bone Lick. The port was a hub of activity for shipping goods and bringing people in to visit the spring and stay at the Clay Hotel and, in later years, the Big Bone Hotel.

Above Left: An attractive Hamilton View
Below Left: A deserted home in Hamilton

Ohio River View

Showboats were a popular attraction at the landing, as travelling performers stopped at the various ports on the river to entertain the residents.

Like the rest of the river towns, diminishing importance of the river took its toll on Hamilton and its neighbouring inland communities of Normansville and Big Bone.

The advance scouts of the Confederate army, from an encampment near Snow's Pond, visited the town in 1862, only to find that several troop transports of Union soldiers had camped there the night before, and were gone already. This was Hamilton's moment of attention by the opposing sides in that conflict. The fortunes of the town were closely linked with that of neighbouring Big Bone.

With the damming of the Ohio River, Hamilton lost riverfront property, where thriving businesses and homes once stood. There are at the present time only a few houses on the site of the town.

Photographs and amended text – Bridget Striker

Concordia Mill. Photograph by Freekee

HAMILTON, OZAUKEE COUNTY, WISCONSIN, 1847

Settled by Irish immigrants "New Dublin" was renamed in 1847 after William S. Hamilton, son of Alexander, spent the night here at what became the first stagecoach stop between Milwaukee and Green Bay (1848). Settled before Cedarburg, Hamilton retains some original buildings including Concordia Mill (1853) and Turner Hall (1867) built by Edward H. Janssen, later Wisconsin State Treasurer. His home also remains.

The Hamilton Turnhalle, a fieldstone building trimmed with cut limestone quoins, lintels and sills, was constructed by local farmers and merchants in 1867.

The last remaining Turner Hall of its type in the United States, it served as a combination meeting place and gymnasium for members of the Hamilton "Turnverein" Society for more than twenty years.

Cedar Creek. Photograph by BaronLarf

When the Society disbanded, the building saw use as a shoe factory and later as a cider mill; however, neither use proved to be economically feasible and the building fell into disrepair. The Turnhalle was entered on the National Register of Historic Places on July 1, 1976. It was donated to the Town of Cedarburg and the Cedarburg Landmark Preservation Society by Adelaide B. Mill. Funds for restoration were provided by a combination of donations from local citizens and a matching grant from the National Park Service obtained through the State Historical Society of Wisconsin.

Even though the dam in Cedar Creek was removed a few years ago and the mill race is now dry, the mill still stands as a monument to the endeavours of industrious Wisconsin pioneers.

WILLIAM S HAMILTON (1797 – 1850)

William S Hamilton

William Stephen Hamilton, a son of Alexander Hamilton and Elizabeth Schuyler Hamilton, was a politician and miner who lived much of his life in the state of Illinois and territorial Wisconsin. Hamilton was born in New York, where he attended the United States Military Academy before he resigned and moved to Illinois in 1817. In Illinois he lived in Springfield and Peoria and eventually migrated to the lead-mining region of southern Wisconsin and established Hamilton's Diggings at present-day Wiota. Hamilton served in various political offices and as a commander in two Midwest Indian Wars. In 1849 he moved to California on the heels of the California Gold Rush. He died in Sacramento, most likely of cholera, in October 1850.

HAMILTON, BUTTE COUNTY, CALIFORNIA, 1848

Hamilton is a former settlement in Butte County, California, and was its first permanent county seat. It was located on the west side of the Feather River, 15 miles downstream from Oroville.

John Bidwell discovered gold at Hamilton in 1848, and the settlement arose. The place was named Hamilton in honour of the nephew of Alexander Hamilton who laid out the town.

Hamilton became the county seat in 1850, after Chico had been the county seat for approximately six weeks based on a provision in the 1850 statute creating Butte County.

The former mining town of Hamilton contained two taverns, one store, and one blacksmith shop. Before long, another tavern was erected, also a new store, forcing the original one to give up business. The clerk's office was situated in the bedroom of Tom Gray's hotel, until a suitable office could be built. Most of the other officers held their offices in their bedrooms of the hotel where they were boarding.

A property tax of one-quarter cent was levied to pay for a courthouse and jail, and after much back-room dealing and bribery, a $9,200 jail was erected. Considering the short period of its use, the cost was hardly worthwhile. It was a first-class jail, however, for that time. The walls were of great solidity and thickness, and so protected with sheet-iron that a prisoner once incarcerated within one of its two gloomy cells left all hope of escape behind until liberated by due process of law. A house sitting about four miles downstream was bought as a new Courthouse and moved up to Hamilton.

As soon as Butte had its courthouse and jail, however, the citizens of Bidwell's Bar (near Oroville, California) got the legislature to declare that their town, and not Hamilton, was the County seat, on the condition that the citizens of Bidwell's Bar build a new courthouse and jail, which they did, and the county seat was moved upstream on August 10, 1853. The "old" courthouse in Hamilton was demolished for its stone, while the jail was put to use as a granary until it burned down in 1878.

A post office was established in 1851 and closed in 1865.

All that is visible from this old town is an overgrown cemetery and the pillars of an old bridge.

Cemetery at Hamilton, Butte County. Photograph by Kimberlee Wheeler

HAMILTON TOWNSHIP, LAWRENCE COUNTY, OHIO, 1850

A rather more modern Hanging Rock. Photograph by mac4run

The village of Hanging Rock, in Hamilton Township once a teeming populated area and the forerunner of the present city of Ironton, was the loading centre for the iron furnaces throughout the county.

The Hanging Rock Iron Region covered an area of more than 1,000 square miles extending into the states of Kentucky and West Virginia and through the counties of Lawrence, Vinton, Scioto, and Jackson in Ohio.

In 1825, the iron region was "almost a wilderness." In 1845 there were 21 furnaces operating in the Ohio section of the district. In 1884 there were some 42 furnaces in the same district.

Hamilton Township was a part of Upper Township in 1850, until the later part of the year, when it was divided into a separate entity.

In 1846, according to historical reports, Hanging Rock, which was about 17 miles downriver from the county seat of Burlington, had a church, four stores, a forge, a rolling mill, a foundry, and approximately 150 inhabitants.

The town grew at a rapid pace because of the booming iron industry and its strategic river location and has been nearly forced into obliteration for the same reasons. A four-lane high way and a complex cloverleaf system near the main part of the village have pushed the town into a small area against the hillside and on the river bank.

Information concerning the naming of the village of Hanging Rock is sketchy and conflicting in many instances. Some historians say that the village was named for the 400-foot-high cliff of sandstone which once hung from the side of the hill, and others state that old river captains named the village after many riverboats were foundered on rocks beneath the surface of the river during summers when the water was low.

The first steam locomotive which ran on the rails, "The Shawnee," was put into operation in 1848.

Robert Hamilton, after whom the township was named, and Andrew Ellison were capitalists who controlled many furnace interests in the area. The two men, according to many reports, built the Pine Grove furnace and other furnaces. Although Pine Grove furnace was in Elizabeth Township, Hamilton, during his later years resided in a stone showplace on the riverbank in Hanging Rock.

Robert Hamilton, listed on the Elizabeth Township records of the 1850 census as "Robert Hamilton, born in Pennsylvania and owning $80,000 worth of property," was "the richest man in Elizabeth Township." He married Nancy Ellison, an "aunt" of Mrs John Campbell, wife of the founder and leading capitalist of Ironton.

He later gained sole propriety of Pine Grove furnace, according to some historical data, and being a very religious man, sought to bring Christian ideals into the Iron industry.

He was supposedly the first iron master in the nation to shut down his furnaces on the Sabbath. Mr Hamilton was also one of the founders of the "Church of Hanging Rock and Pine Grove," which still stands on the main corner of the village, near the post office. The church, dedicated on November 23, 1850, is still in use and is the oldest occupied public building in the county.

From the days of the three-mile railroad into the hills through the glory of the Hanging Rock Region and now the expressway U.S. 52, Hamilton Township has played an important part in county and state history, due to its strategic position on the riverfront. Today the eastern sector of the township contains a small part of the city of Ironton.

HAMILTON, LA CROSSE COUNTY, WISCONSIN, 1851

A Hamilton, Wisconsin View. Photograph by Magnit

Hamilton is a town in La Crosse County, Wisconsin. It lies on the La Crosse River and many of the original settlers were Norwegian.

The Town of Hamilton was named by John M. Coburn, after Hamilton College in Clinton, New York. The population was 2,301 at the 2000 Census.

HAMILTON FORT, IRON COUNTY, UTAH, 1852

Photograph by Daniel Ter-Nedden at ghosttowngallery.com

Hamilton Fort is four miles south of Cedar City in Iron County, Utah. The settlement was founded in 1852 and known as Shirts Creek after the creek near where the fort stood. The fort and creek were both named for Peter Shirts, a noted Mormon pioneer and scout. After the Indian wars of 1853, Shirts sold the fort and his land to his neighbour, John Hamilton. At that time it was known as Fort Walker, supposedly in honour of the noted Indian Chief Walker. It was during the Indian wars with Chief Walker that the settlers moved out and into nearby Cedar City. When the settlers returned in 1857 they renamed the settlement Sidon "after the Phoenician City of Asia." In 1869 the settlers moved half a mile north of the old fort and renamed the site Hamilton in honour of John Hamilton. It is now a ghost town.

Photographs by Daniel Ter-Nedden at ghosttowngallery.com

Hamilton City Hall. Photograph by Bruce Wicks

HAMILTON, HANCOCK COUNTY, ILLINOIS, 1854

Hamilton was laid out in 1852 by several men in the area, including Samuel Gordon, who furnished a 160-acre tract of land on the banks of the Mississippi River. This land was purchased in 1833 by his father, John, for $150.

Artois Hamilton, of Carthage, was also active in the early history of the town. He was an hotelier in Carthage, Illinois but very little is known of him other than he was lucky to survive a Cholera epidemic which claimed a number of members of his family in July 1851. Mr Hamilton was thought to hold money bags of considerable size, so the new town was named "Hamilton", in the hope that the honour might induce him to finance the town. Other names were presented and discussed, including Bartlett, Rapids City and East Keokuk, but the possible contribution of money was the clear winner in identifying a name for the town.

Hamilton was officially incorporated as a town in 1854, and then re-incorporated as a city in 1859.

Hamilton Post Office. Photograph by Bruce Wicks

Not much is known about Hamilton's population in the early years, but it is known to have stood at 1,200 in 1831 and 1,800 in 1893.

Back in the early 1900's, it was not uncommon to see cattle crossing the Keokuk - Hamilton Bridge. A gentleman by the name of Mr Hyndman drove large herds of cattle across the bridge to Missouri. Before the structure was built, a ferry boat transported folks across the river. In 1871 a single deck bridge was built which was to be used for vehicular, railroad, and wagon traffic. There was also a toll house at each end of the bridge, just in case Mr Hyndman and his cows wanted to go west as a train was planning an easterly trip across the bridge.

Built at a cost of $1,005,000, the huge iron structure was a project of the Keystone Bridge Company of Pittsburgh. President of this company was Andrew Carnegie of New York. Opened to the public in June, 1871, it was constructed entirely of iron, except the road bed, which was of heavy-sawed white-oak lumber. It took nearly two years to build, delayed several times by ice and high water. The bridge was 2,194 feet long, and rested on eleven stone piers. Its draw, for the passage of steamboats and other river craft, was 378 feet in length, turned by steam machinery on a pivot in the centre.

The great bridge met with a mishap on November 4, 1881, when the steamer War Eagle was swept downstream and collided with a pier. An emergency span was needed while a new, permanent span was being constructed. The "emergency span" was what came to be known as the old Hamilton covered bridge. The cost of damage to the bridge by the War Eagle was $150,000, and to the boat itself, was $50,000.

The idea of covered bridges was brought to America from Europe in the early 1800's. The roofs on the bridges were practical notions, as protection for the wooden spans. At one time 10,000 of these structures dotted the U.S., but by 1960 the number had dwindled to approximately 1,000. At 169 feet, the longest covered bridge in Illinois was the historic bridge in Hamilton. Tragically, the bridge was destroyed by fire in the summer of 1969. Used for two years until a permanent replacement was constructed, the covered bridge was then moved across a slough of the Mississippi River. This was at the entrance to a road that was parallel to the dike to the Mississippi River Bridge. The wooden span had been taken carefully apart and transported by barge where it was reassembled at its new location.

A new roadway was built from Hamilton to the Mississippi River Bridge in 1955, which then by-passed the covered bridge and winding road. At this time, the bridge and surrounding land became the property of the State of Illinois, and was then used for pedestrian traffic only. Situated at the foot of Main Street, the old covered bridge was the approach to Montebello Recreation Area. Prior to 1955, it is said that this was the only covered bridge to carry heavy inter-state traffic, as other bridges were located in rural areas.

In the early 1900's, it was determined that something was needed to aid river navigation and harness the wealth of water power inherent in the mighty Mississippi. A bill was introduced in 1904 which granted the Keokuk and Hamilton Water Power Company the right to construct a dam across the river at the foot of the rapids. A year later, Hugh L. Cooper, a hydro-electric engineer, took an option to build the dam for $20,000,000. The proportions of this lock and dam were immense.

There were some delays in the construction of the lock and dam (namely, flooded cofferdams and ice build ups) however, the project was completed on schedule, and the opening of the locks was heralded with two riverboats passing through the locks together on June 12, 1913. Electricity was transmitted to St. Louis on June 30, 1913,

Hamilton-Keokuk Bridge. Photograph by Madmaxmarchhare

Hotel Granite, Hamilton. Photograph by Bruce Wicks

and the project was completed.

Between 1887 and 1936, forty five new buildings were erected, with business on Main Street thriving. Hamilton's other business district was (and is now) located on Broadway. There were many stores open for business during this era, including a drugstore/soda fountain, Waggoner's jewellery store, the Springfield Coal, Lime and Cement Company, and B.W. Elder's Sale Barn (for horse and mule auction sales). Gray's Store, which handled dry goods, was the "home" of the post office in the 1890's, and the sidewalks were literally "board" walks.

The 1912 City Directory reflects a booming town, with a multitude of businesses and services available. In that year, Hamilton boasted ten factories, and no less than eight grocery stores. The town was also served by two newspapers -the Hamilton Press and the Hamilton Tribune.

Many other establishments lined the town streets, reflecting industries as diverse as buggies and carriage repair to tailors and millinery. The town was served by numerous attorneys, bankers, blacksmiths and barbers. For the sweet tooth, there were bakeries and confectioners, to complement the meat markets and Denton's dairy. Out-of-towners could choose from three hotels for respite, and all could enjoy a picture show at The Gem Theatre.

Between 1905 and 1926, people came from miles around to attend the Chautauqua's, which were cultural events, lectures, recitals, and music. The ten day events were held at Wildcat Springs, and Gordon's Grove, which is now part of City Park.

Wildcat Springs, a spacious and sprawling tract of land, is located on the north side of Hamilton. It has been a popular recreation area since the 1880's and remains so today with camping, hiking, and picnicking facilities. Its name is derived from a legend that the last wildcat in the area was killed there. Today, a lucky visitor can still spot a bobcat and hear their shrill cries in the night. Chaney Creek, which flows through Wildcat Springs Park, is a popular place to hunt for geodes.

Quartz is mined at Gray's mine in the town.

Hamilton remains a quaint river community with many opportunities.

One of Hamilton's Older Houses. Photograph by Bruce Wicks

One of Hamilton's Churches. Photograph by Bruce Wicks

95

The Boone River in Hamilton County. Photograph by Tim Kiser

A waterfall in Hamilton County. Photograph by Catherine Bergman

HAMILTON COUNTY, IOWA, 1857

The beginning of Hamilton County, Iowa as we know it today can be told from the time this region was inhabited by the Sac and Fox Indian tribes. The mighty Sioux Indians lived to the north and the two groups were continually at war with each other. The Federal Government attempted to separate the groups by constructing a neutral strip of land 40 miles wide that cut diagonally through the area, the southern boundary of which passed through what was to become Hamilton County. The Indians were reimbursed 3¢ per acre for this land in 1830.

The first settler was Jasper Bell who had followed the Des Moines River as far as the east fork (later renamed the Boone River). This was before Hamilton was a county.

Iowa was organized as a state in 1846 with only a few counties, but by 1850 the number of counties had grown to fifty. Risley, named for a Colonel in the Mexican War, was organized as the county for the area, but there were no towns and no county seat. The county was administered by Boone County to the south, but by 1852 Hook's Point had become the principal trading point in the county. Granville Burkley came and worked as the first school teacher. During a two-week recess in 1852 he travelled through Risley, and the county to the west named Yell, to get signatures on a petition to have the two counties joined as one. There were only about 50 people living in the two counties at the time. A prominent legislator had the bill changed and Yell was re-named Webster County.

In the mid-1850s Homer grew in size. It had a post office, school, lawyer's office and stage line. In 1857 a call for an election to move the county seat to Fort Dodge

Cruise to the woods – A car rally in Hamilton County.
Photograph by Catherine Bergman

Windfarm at dusk outside Blairsburg, Hamilton County.
Photograph by Jesse Derber

Hamilton County Courthouse, Webster City

was considered. The results of a very dubious election resulted in the removal of the county seat to Fort Dodge. Locals tell of a wrestling match that was held to determine the county seat. In the end the one large county was re-split into two. One part became Webster County with Fort Dodge as the county seat while the other part, Risley, was renamed Hamilton in honour of the President of the Iowa senate. The county seat was Newcastle – later renamed Webster City.

Hamilton County today is considered rural by any standards with a population of about 16,000 and a strong agricultural heritage. Primary industries in 2012 are education and manufacturing, which make up about 40% of the workforce. However, with the 2011 closure of Webster City's largest employer (a manufacturer of washing machines and dryers) the economy has entered a slump. More than half of the county's residents live in Webster City. The remainder are spread across the rural areas and eight small towns. Many residents commute to work in nearby larger towns. Recreation is important to the county as it is has two good-sized rivers flowing through it. The green belt area is known across the state for good canoeing and fishing. The county park system has many appealing amenities including campgrounds, fishing, picnicking, playgrounds, cabins, a youth hunting area, and other educational areas.

Text – Catherine Bergman

Family Fishing Outing at Ellsworth, Hamilton County. Photograph by Laura Nott

HAMILTON CITY AND COUNTY, TEXAS, 1858

Indigenous peoples were the first inhabitants of the area. Later Indian tribes settled in the area, including Tawakoni, Tonkawa, Waco and Comanche.

In 1821, shortly after Mexico claimed its independence from Spain, Anglo settlers from the North came to Texas, claiming Mexican citizenship.

Following Texas's independence from Mexico (1836) and its annexation by the United States (1845), Robert Carter and family became the first permanent white settlers in the county in 1854. The next year, settlers James Rice, Henry Standefer, Frederic Bookerman, William Beauchamp, and Asa Langford formed a community that later became the town of Hamilton. Asa Langford began Langford's Cove, which later grew into present-day Evant. In 1856 the Sixth Texas Legislature formed Hamilton County from parts of Comanche, Bosque and Lampas Counties and was named after James Hamilton Jr., a former governor of South Carolina who gave financial aid to the Republic of Texas. In 1858, Hamilton was named the county seat.

Despite growing white settlements in Texas, Indian tribal presences remained. In 1867, Comanche raiders attacked a school where Ann Whitney was the teacher. She helped students escape before finally succumbing to eighteen Comanche arrows.

By 1900, cotton cultivation had spread to almost 47,500 acres of county land. By 1907, the Stephenville, North and South Texas Railway had connected Hamilton with Stephenville. The St. Louis Southwestern Railway of Texas connected Hamilton with Comanche.

Above Right: Main Street in Hico, Hamilton County. Photograph by Billy Hathorn
Below Right: Hamilton County Courthouse. Photograph by Steve Almquist

Hamilton County is located on the Edwards Plateau in Central Texas. It boasts rolling prairies, cultivated farmlands, tree-shaded rivers and creeks flowing through hills and valleys as well as small, rural communities. Agriculture continues to play a major role in the economy of the County but, in addition, a full range of retail businesses, specialty shops, some featuring locally produced merchandise, and professional offices flourish. The County produces limited oil, gas and gravel.

Sheltered in a pleasant valley of Pecan Creek, the City of Hamilton delights home folks and visitors alike with its scenic beauty every season of the year. Lovely trees, historic homes and buildings surround the majestic Hamilton County Courthouse, the centre of life and commerce of the community.

The City has three parks with a total of 60 acres. One of them, Pecan Creek Park, a linear greenbelt, meanders ten blocks through downtown Hamilton.

Hamilton's moderate climate affords the possibility of year-round fishing, boating and other water sports at City Lake, Cowhouse Creek, Leon River and nearby Lake Proctor. Deer, quail, dove, duck and turkey hunting draws hunters to Hamilton from early September through early spring. Small game hunting for rabbit, fox, squirrel, bobcat and raccoon is also conveniently available. The annual Hamilton County Dove Festival celebrates the opening of dove season with a city-wide event reminiscent of an old-fashioned county fair and rodeo. Held in early September, the Dove Festival attracts about 5,000 visitors to Hamilton.

The highly acclaimed Hamilton Civic Theatre performs five live shows each year beginning in the spring and ending with a children's Christmas pageant. Under on-going renovation, the Hamilton Fine Arts Centre houses exhibits, seminars, art and dance classes and more.

There are more than 40 active local civic organizations serving a variety of age groups, community needs, educational and recreational interests.

The motto for the city is "Hamilton, what a hometown should be."

Above Right: Hamilton General Hospital. Photograph by Steve Almquist
Below Right: Statue of Billy the Kid in Hico, Hamilton County.
Photograph by Michael Bilodeau
Text – Steve Almquist

St Mary's Episcopal Church. Photograph by Michael Bilodeau

Welcome Sign to Hamilton Missouri. Photograph by J Stephen Conn

HAMILTON, CALDWELL COUNTY, MISSOURI, 1859

Hamilton, which is the largest town in Caldwell County, was founded in 1859 along the route of the Hannibal and St. Joseph Railroad. It was founded by Albert Gallatin Davis and named for Alexander Hamilton and Joseph Hamilton.

Signs of the Victorian town are still visible today. Hamilton's business community offers a variety of retail and service businesses, as well as antique shops and malls. Many services and activities make this small town attractive to its residents and visitors. They include an AAA rated school system, the Hamilton Public Library, Hamilton Community Arts Theatre, a new swimming pool, 9-hole golf course, several churches, medical clinics and two major festivals held each year.

J.C.Penney's boyhood home – Now a museum

Hamilton has the distinction of being the birthplace and boyhood home of James Cash Penney (J.C. Penney) who was born September 16, 1875. He established a chain of department stores across the nation and used the old fashioned values he learned in Hamilton as a foundation for his business and personal life. He always maintained a close relationship with his hometown. Penney donated funds to help build the first library, the shoe factory, the high school, Highland Cemetery and the American Legion Park. Today Hamilton has a beautiful museum that houses a public library and a well-used community room, as well as his boyhood home.

Lick Observatory atop Mount Hamilton. Photograph by Edward Rooks

MOUNT HAMILTON, SANTA CLARA COUNTY, CALIFORNIA, 1861

Looking North from Mount Hamilton. Photograph by Eric Schneider

Mount Hamilton is a 4,196 feet mountain peak near Morgan Hill, California.

On August 26, 1861, while working for Josiah D. Whitney on the first California Geological Survey, William H. Brewer invited local San Jose preacher (and Brewer's personal friend) Laurentine Hamilton to join his company on a trek to a nearby summit. Nearing the completion of their journey, Hamilton, in good humour, bounded for the summit ahead of the rest of the men and claimed his stake.

Mount Hamilton is the tallest mountain overlooking Silicon Valley, and is the site of Lick Observatory, the first permanently occupied mountain-top observatory.

Golden Eagle nesting sites are found on the mountain.

LAURENTINE HAMILTON (1826 – 1882)

Laurentine Hamilton was a Presbyterian minister accused of heresy, and founder of the First Unitarian Church of Oakland.

Hamilton was born in Catlin, New York, near Seneca Lake. He graduated from Hamilton College in Clinton, New York in 1850 and went on to attend Auburn Theological Seminary, from which he graduated in 1853. In 1854 Hamilton became an ordained minister of the Presbyterian Church in Ovid, New York.

In 1855 he was assigned as pastor of Columbia, California, a small mining camp established during the California Gold Rush, where he built the Presbyterian Church that still stands. In 1859 Hamilton came to San Jose, California to preach at the First Presbyterian Church of San Jose. He became Superintendent of San Jose Schools, and in 1861 he travelled with William H. Brewer and Charles F. Hoffmann to the summit of a nearby mountain, as part of the initial California Geological Survey. Mount Hamilton, is named after him.

In 1864 Hamilton became pastor of the First Presbyterian Church of Oakland, his sermons appearing in the Oakland Daily Tribune. He served on the Oakland Board of Education from 1866 to 1872. In 1869, Hamilton came under scrutiny for teaching the doctrine of "a second probation after death" (stating one has a second, posthumous chance of salvation). He was charged with heresy and forced to leave his pastorate and resign from his ordination in the Presbyterian Church. Most of his parishioners joined him in forming the First Independent Presbyterian Church, later to become the Independent Church of Oakland. In 1879 the church joined the American Unitarian Association and became the First Unitarian Church of Oakland.

While preaching on Easter Sunday, 1882, Hamilton spoke "We know not what matter is..." and then collapsed onto the ground, dead.

Bust of Laurentine Hamilton at Lick Observatory (Mt. Hamilton)

Above: Streeter – Peterson House, Aurora. Photograph by Ammodramus.
Right: Hamilton County Courthouse, Aurora. Photograph by K.Johnson

HAMILTON COUNTY, NEBRASKA, 1867

In 1861, David Millspaw became the first permanent settler in the area of what was to become Aurora. Hamilton County was formed in 1867 and was named after Alexander Hamilton, the first Secretary of the Treasury. Voters elected to move the county seat to Aurora in 1875. In 2010, the population was 9,124.

Early migration routes to and from Hamilton County, for European and African American settlers included: the Oregon Trail in 1830s to 1890s from western Missouri to Oregon City, Oregon; the California Trail 1846 to 1869 from western Missouri to northern California; the Mormon Trail 1846 to 1869 from Nauvoo, Illinois to Salt Lake City, Utah.

St John's Evangelical Lutheran Church, Kronborg. Photograph by Ammodramus.

Explorit Centre. Photograph by M Lanka

Today Hamilton sits amidst the open spaces of land and sky known as the Great Plains, far from the noise and crowds of large cities. This is America's heartland, where the products that feed and fuel the world are produced and the charm of rural America is still intact.

Aurora, the county seat, is a vibrant community proud of its agricultural-based heritage and is poised for dynamic growth with an eye towards technology. Aurora has something for everyone. No matter what you're looking for, you'll find it here.

The Edgerton Explorit Centre, a tribute to Harold "Doc" Edgerton, is "Nebraska's

The main street of Hampton village, Hamilton County. Photograph by Publichall

Hands-on Science Centre." Its exhibits and activities educate and entertain people of all ages. Directly next door the Plainsman Museum tells the history of Hamilton County and the Great Plains.

Aurora's Central Park Square is the hub of the city's retail industry and the historic Hamilton County Courthouse is also in this area.

On June 22, 2003 Aurora was the site of the second largest hailstone ever recorded.

HAMILTON CITY, FREMONT COUNTY, WYOMING, 1868

"Gold!" Prospectors discovered the rich lode known as a miner's delight in September 1867 at the southern tip of the Wind River Mountains, Dakota Territory. At a gold-feverish pace the men began full-scale mining at the Miner's Delight Mine in 1868, the year Wyoming Territory was carved out of Dakota. The nearby town became Hamilton City, but no one appears to have documented for whom, by whom, or why.

Chicago reporter James Chisholm said the town is, "A number of log houses nestled snugly enough near a field of young trees and bushes. " Upon returning from mining men would light wood stoves in their cabins and eat suppers of elk or antelope. They did not work Sundays when pastimes were card playing and drinking. Though the town was a quiet mountain camp Chisholm admitted, "A vast amount of the gold dust is ground in the whisky mill." One miner had a grizzly bear cub as a pet. Of the four women, only one, Candy, had a "reputation." Candy later married an owner of Miner's Delight and became "mistress of his mud covered cabin."

Indian attacks were a constant threat. In 1869 Arapahos killed John G. Anderson before being driven off by Army soldiers. In 1870 newlyweds Margaret and Michael Heenan joined the growing community to seek their fortune. Sioux ambushed Michael as he hauled hay for his mules. Three days later the widowed Margaret gave birth to a daughter. The attacks ceased in 1872 when the tribes signed a treaty granting the land to the U.S. Government.

At its 1870 apex Hamilton City's census reflected 75 inhabitants. Of those 40 were miners. Other occupations included a liquor dealer, a plumber, and a shoemaker. The census reveals the ladies were wives. No members of the "ancient profession" were represented.

Right: Bryant Cabin with its lean-to, drive-through structure that was wide enough for freight wagons of the day to make deliveries. A table inside the lean-to's short exterior wall holds cans, glass chards, and other rusty, broken memorabilia found by visitors to Hamilton City.

Few artefacts remain, but this wood-fired cook stove's skeleton endures the elements outside one of the remaining cabins at Hamilton City.

Beaver pond is a stone's throw east of Hamilton City, Wyo. A path to the right of the pond leads to the Hamilton City / Miner's Delight cemetery.

As a gold-boom town Hamilton City would never enjoy a permanent population. In its early years the Miner's Delight Mine produced gold valued between $60,000 and $70,000. Venture capitalists poured in money and equipment, but within ten years the mine had busted.

Hamilton City underwent a good many transitions in its short life. It was one of scores of Old West towns abandoned when rumours of the next gold rush beckoned miners to another place. Three counties—Carter, Sweetwater, and Fremont—governed the town as populations and political boundaries shifted on the frontier. In 1890 Wyoming gained statehood and Hamilton City was secure in Fremont County. The town's original buildings are gone, but another short-lived gold boom in 1907 left behind the existing saloon and a dozen other log and plank cabins.

Five miles southwest of Hamilton City (more commonly known today as Miner's Delight) sits Atlantic City, another 1868 gold-boom town. Long-time Atlanticans tell of recluses secretly living at Miner's Delight as recently as the 1990s. Listed on The National Register of Historic Places, Hamilton City (Miner's Delight) attracts locals, historians, tourists checking ghost towns off their life lists, and select wayfarers sent by locals to enjoy the serenity.

Sage brush landscapes the eastern outskirts of Hamilton City. Limestone Mountain stands watch from the north. Pine and aspen reclaim cabins and other remnants of the town. From within weather-blackened cabins chattering squirrels on buckled floors warn visitors to keep out. Through open doors and missing windows the winds have robbed the cabins of their secrets.

The town's cemetery is a short walk past a beaver pond, up a steep footpath through a pine forest, to the top of a wind-blown knoll. Anna Atherton's headstone stands alone amid iron-fenced depressions of other graves. Anna arrived in this world in 1837 and departed it in 1875. An anonymous caretaker adorns Anna's plot with flowers through the summer months. Other markers—probably wood—have not survived the elements at the cemetery's 8,280 feet.

'tis quiet now, but Hamilton City, Wyoming, conjures every ghost the Old West knew. Gold miners, Indians, soldiers, pioneers, fur trappers, blacksmiths, stage drivers, saloon keepers, cowboys, ladies, shop keepers, and others crossed paths here.

Photographs and text - Barbara and Bob Townsend – Hosts of Miner's Delight B&B

HAMILTON, WHITE PINE COUNTY, NEVADA, 1868

Hamilton is an abandoned mining town located in the White Pine Range, in western White Pine County, Nevada.

In 1868 silver ore was discovered near Hamilton and 25,000 people of all types migrated to the area. Hamilton became the first county seat of White Pine County in 1869. The boom lasted until 1887 when large scale production ceased as all the silver was found on top of the surface and there was none below. At 8,000 feet elevation, people weren't about to stay to see if a real vein could be located. People moved out almost at the same rate as they moved in. By then there had been shipped a total of $22,000,000 in silver bullion. At this time Hamilton lost its place as county seat to the town of Ely.

Treasure Hill was the site of silver discoveries in late 1867. The area was not suitable for a town site, so one was located at the base of Treasure Hill in May of 1868. The town was given its name after a W. H. Hamilton, one of the three men that laid out the town site. By June, the town had a population of 30 and one business establishment—a saloon. Rich discoveries on Treasure Hill created a boom and a huge rush to Hamilton took place. By winter, Hamilton's population had swelled to 600. Once the spring thaw was over, the town had a floating population of over 10,000. Stage lines were running to Hamilton on a regular basis by summer. When White Pine County was organized in March of 1869, Hamilton was selected as the county seat. By summer, Hamilton boasted a population of 12,000. There were close to 100 saloons, several breweries, 60 general stores, and many other businesses. The town also had theatres, dance halls, skating rinks, a Miners' Union Hall, and a fraternal order. During the peak of the White Pine rush, close to 200 mining companies were operating in the area and 25,000 people were living in the vicinity.

Photographs by Rick Pisio www.rwphotos.com

However, once the uncertainty of the mines' potential became known, many of the prospectors left the district. Hamilton then experienced a depression and many residents left as quickly as they had come. The population shrunk to 3,915. A disastrous fire on June 27, 1873 spread throughout the business district and caused $600,000 in damage. Hamilton's slide continued and by late 1873 the population had dwindled to 500. Another fire struck the town on January 5, 1885, destroying the courthouse and much of what remained in the dying town. Hamilton was dealt its worst blow when the county seat was moved to Ely in 1887. The town was revived in the early 1980s when extensive mining operations began on Treasure Hill. The town now has about 75 residents and care has been taken not to disturb the ruins.

Trestle Bridge near Hamilton, Allegan Township.
Photograph by Susanne Garvelink

HAMILTON, ALLEGAN TOWNSHIP, MICHIGAN, 1870

Hamilton is an unincorporated community in the northeast corner of Heath Township, on the Rabbit River. The first white settler was Charles Butler, who purchased the entirety of section 6 in 1835. It was first known as Rabbit River, with a post office operating from May 1851 to September 1852. Aaron Willards platted a village named Rabbit River in 1862, with a second post office opening in July 1864. The post office was renamed "Hamilton" in May 1870.

HAMILTON TOWNSHIP, TIOGA COUNTY, PENNSYLVANIA, 1871

On December 7th 1871 the township of Hamilton was formed from the townships of Bloss and Ward. At the time of its formation all the inhabitants were in the village of Morris Run, which is about two and a half miles east of Blossburg, on the head waters of a creek bearing the name of Morris Run, which empties into the Tioga River one and a half miles southeast of Blossburg.

In 1852 explorations for coal were made on the west side of the creek by the Tioga Improvement Company, whose officers and stockholders were chiefly residents of Philadelphia. During that year, under the direction of the company, Colonel Pharon Jarrett, of Lock Haven, Pennsylvania assisted by H. Brewer and J. Livingston, surveyed a route for a railroad from Blossburg to where the coal cropped out, and where the "openings" had been made. This railroad was finally constructed and opened for the transportation of coal in October 1853. The business of the company was carried on for about ten years, by which time there had been 323,174 tons mined, or an average of about 30,000 tons annually. The mine changed hands and continued to grow. By 1880 the local population had passed 2,000.

The township now has a population of around 450 largely living in Morris Run.

Above Left: Northern entrance to Township
Above Centre: Fishing Club Sign
Above Right: Industrial Area
Photographs by James Tutak

HAMILTON COUNTY, KANSAS, 1873

Hamilton County was named after Alexander Hamilton. The county is located in the southwest part of Kansas, and contains an area of 996 square miles. Located within the Great Plains, the county is relatively level, mostly treeless, and semi-arid. It receives an annual precipitation of 17 inches. The prevailing winds are southerly, except during the winter months. The population in 1990 was 2,388.

Eighty seven per cent of the land area is used for agriculture. Livestock ranked first in value production, with four commercial feedlots currently in operation. The world's largest beef-packing plant is located fifty miles east of Hamilton County, which is the major reason the cattle business is prominent. Wheat ranked second in value production, and is the major crop, followed by hay, corn, and sorghum. Irrigation plays a prominent role in the agricultural economy.

The County consists of three communities, Kendall, Coolidge, and Syracuse, the county seat. In the 1880's the county had more than thirty school districts. The number has dwindled to one school district located in Syracuse.

The Santa Fe Trail, an ancient route, was used regularly after 1821 by merchant traders travelling to Santa Fe, New Mexico. It followed the Arkansas River through Hamilton County. The importance of the trail faded with the coming of the railroad in the early 1870s.

A stage coach station was located in Hamilton County at Spring Creek. It was formally established as a fort in September of 1865, and named after Francis Xavier Aubry. Fort Aubry was built because of the need for protection on the Santa Fe Trail from Indians and renegades, although major battles were never recorded at the fort. The troops lived in sod buildings and dug-outs. The number of troops stationed at Fort Aubry reached its peak in December 1865 with 363 soldiers. By April of 1866, after only seven months of operations as a fort, Fort Aubry was deactivated.

With the construction of the Atchison-Topeka and Santa Fe Railroad in 1871-72 through Hamilton County, came a wave of advertising by the railroad to convince people to homestead in Kansas. A group of people from Syracuse, New York decided to scout out the area. They found the land of Hamilton County to hold countless possibilities, and convinced 25 to 40 families to settle there. The railroad offered to move the settlers free of charge and if they were dissatisfied, would move them elsewhere.

Monument to Santa Fe Trail in Coolidge. Photograph by Billy Hathorn

At that time, Syracuse consisted of a side track and a water tower and was called Hollidaysburg, named after C.K. Holliday, President of the railroad. The group arrived at Hollidaysburg in March of 1873 and soon after the townspeople decided to change the name of the town to Syracuse, in honour of their hometown.

They built homes of sod and imported lumber. The first home built of lumber was constructed by President of the colony, E.P. Barber. It served as a home and also as a refuge for the townspeople during the Indian Scares. The house, which still stands, is preserved by the Hamilton County Historical Society.

The crops planted by the settlers were not suited to the Kansas climate and, adversely affected by a drought and Rocky Mountain locust plague, the first crop failed. Many of the colonists became discouraged and took the railroad up on their offer to move them elsewhere. By 1884, only three of the original settlers remained, E.P. Barber, James Gates, and H.N. Lester, founder of the local newspaper. In the late 1880s, more settlers came to Syracuse from Ohio and Illinois and the county experienced a boom.

Coolidge, a town fourteen miles west of Syracuse, also came about due to the railroad and was named after T.J. Coolidge, President of the railroad. The Santa Fe Railroad used Coolidge as a base of operations, which created the need for stores, saloons, stables, and other services. Coolidge was also a division point of the railroad where they would change crew, load up with coal and water as well as greasing and repairing the engines. The town took shape with more businesses being built all the time. One of these was a $75,000 opera house which gave one performance, before it burnt to the ground. Its peak years were 1885-1887. The town was platted in 1886, making it the first organized city in Hamilton County. In the late 1880s, Coolidge enjoyed a huge cattle trade and had a floating population of 800 to 1,000. The division point was moved from Coolidge to La Junta, Colorado, in 1890 and the population began to decline steadily.

Kendall was platted in February, 1885, and by May, 200 houses had been built. The town was originally called Aubry, but was changed to Kendall, after the Kendall brothers who were popular merchants in the area. Kendall was named temporary county seat in 1886, but the seat was moved to Syracuse by a Kansas Supreme Court decision in July 1888. Kendall survived losing the county seat but remains a small unincorporated community.

Today, the communities of Kendall and Coolidge exist with a population of less than 100 each, and Syracuse has a population of 1,623. The people of Hamilton County have survived countless droughts, floods, depressions, blizzards, heat waves, wars, and technological changes. The pages of the past help the citizens of this county to look to tomorrow with continued steadfast determination.

Above Right: Hamilton County Courthouse, Syracuse. Photograph by Ammodramus
Below Right: There's still a Cinema in Syracuse! Photograph by Billy Hathorn

Mural of Cavalry Soldier in Syracuse, Hamilton County, Kansas . Photograph by Billy Hathorn

HAMILTON, GRANT COUNTY, OREGON, 1874

Hamilton is an unincorporated community in Grant County, Oregon. It is located on Oregon Route 402 east of Monument and west of Long Creek. As of 1993, the community had no businesses and only three houses.

The community and nearby Hamilton Mountain were named for John Henry Hamilton,

the first settler in the area. Hamilton, a cattle rancher, arrived in Grant County sometime in 1874 and lived there until his death in 1909. Local settlers met at Hamilton's ranch to race horses. Hamilton post office was established in 1884 and closed in 1959. Anson C. Frink built the first store and served as the first postmaster.

Route 402 as it passes the Old Hamilton Cemetery.
Photograph by P G Holbrook

JOHN HENRY HAMILTON (1826 – 1909)

John Henry Hamilton was born 5 April 1826 in Kentucky, and died 6 December 1909 in Grant, Oregon. In 1848, he married Mary, the daughter of Nathaniel and Nancy Robins of Greenburg, Indiana.

In 1851, they moved to Randolph County, Missouri, spending the winter there before starting across the plains in the spring.

In 1852, they embarked on the Oregon Trail with their extended family, according to the Grant County Museum, family stories and records posted on the Internet. Cholera struck the wagon train and, in a single night, killed three of Mary's sisters in Nebraska or Kansas.

Presumably the Hamiltons travelled with son John, who was born in Illinois. Daughter Mary was born in Indiana.

The Hamiltons settled in the Willamette Valley near Oregon City.

In the spring of 1872, the Hamiltons moved to Grant County's Indian Valley on Deer Creek and being first settlers in the area, the town that grew there was named after them.

Known as Senator Hamilton, John was a lover of fine blooded horses. He owned and raced an outstanding animal, Blue Mountain Bell, which held the record of the best time of all race horses in the Western states. He also owned another popular race horse, Napper, who ran a very fast half mile.

The Grant County Museum called him "one of the most highly respected and esteemed of the early day pioneers."

HAMILTON, LOUDOUN COUNTY, VIRGINIA, 1875

Mount Zion United Methodist Church

Located at the foot of the Catoctin Mountain, in an area once occupied by several native tribes, the present-day Hamilton began as a small settlement about seven miles west of Leesburg and 40 miles northwest of Washington, D.C., in about 1750. George and Tabitha Tavenner lived north of the settlement in a stone house they built in 1788. In the early 1800s one of their sons, Richard, and his wife Ann Hatcher, built a stone and log house which they called Harmony and the surrounding area took on the name. In 1826, Harmony's name was changed to Hamilton's Store when the post office was established, with Charles Bennett Hamilton as postmaster. In 1831 the Leesburg and Snickers Gap Turnpike Company opened a road connecting Leesburg, six miles east of Hamilton, and Snickersville, 12 miles west of Hamilton. The road expanded trade, and growth in the area followed. By December of 1835, Hamilton's Store had become just plain Hamilton, but the village could easily have been named 'Tavennerville', or perhaps 'Laycockville', or 'Rogersville' as many members of these families, too, settled in the area and contributed to its rapid development as an attractive and important village. Many descendants of these families continue to call Hamilton home.

The Town was incorporated by an act of the General Assembly approved February 18, 1875, with John H. Hughes as Mayor. When the Town was incorporated, Hamilton was second in population only to Leesburg, the county seat.

Hamilton's first church, Harmony Methodist Episcopal Church was completed in 1833. After more than 170 years and several renovations and additions, Harmony United Methodist Church remains an active Church and important part of the community.

In addition to Harmony United Methodist Church, the Town's growing population supported the construction of St. Paul's Episcopal Church and on Sunday, March 1, 1874 the Town of Hamilton had its first service by an Episcopal clergyman. Currently the Church is the Church of the Holy Scripture. The Town's third Church, Mount Zion United Methodist Church was established in 1881 for the purpose of providing a place of worship for African Americans. The Church continues to thrive today.

On April 7, 1889, with four inches of snow on the ground, Hamilton's fourth Church, the Hamilton Baptist Church, was founded. Throughout its nearly 125-year history changes, improvements, and building expansions have been made to accommodate its growing congregation.

Hamilton and the surrounding areas having good soil, abundant water supplies and a geography well suited for farming, were largely agrarian. However, to meet the needs of the growing community, craftsmen, mills, tailoring shops, and general supply stores began to spring up.

The first school in Hamilton was built behind the Harmony Methodist Church in the late 1840s. It is not clear when this school fell into disuse, but it has been described as a one-room school which was built on Tavenners' property. In 1869 the Loudoun Valley Academy was established. The school taught Latin, Greek, and higher math. Loudoun Valley Academy closed in 1874 replaced that year by Hamilton's fourth school, in the Masonic Lodge. Built in 1873 the Lodge, now privately owned, has been rewarded with National Trust designation. Today, area children can begin their education at Hamilton Elementary School. Harmony Intermediate School, just outside the Town's corporate limits, serves grades six through eight. High School students attend school in nearby Purcellville or in Leesburg.

Hamilton Baptist Church

Hamilton 1911

Waverly Villa

Janney Hill

While there is considerable debate concerning the ferociousness of the event, no story of Hamilton would be complete without a reference to the "Hamilton Fight" during the American Civil War. On March 21, 1865, Confederate Colonel John S. Mosby and his men engaged a group of Union soldiers led by Colonel Marcus Reno. Although many believe the engagement was little more than a skirmish, the event was the last important action of the American Civil War in Loudoun County. Civil War aficionados still find surviving artefacts from both sides in the area.

In late 1868 the first Washington and Old Dominion (W&OD) Railroads train pulled into Hamilton Station, located a half-mile north of the Town. Hamilton gained prominence and boarding houses accommodated "summer people" escaping the heat and mosquitos of Washington, D.C.. Trotting races and theatricals enlivened weekends, a toll house regulated traffic bound for points west, and businesses grew up on both sides of Hamilton's main street. These businesses became dependent on the railroad for supplies while area farmers were now able to ship their crops and livestock to

Alexandria and Washington. In 1907 Samuel Edgar Rogers bought and enlarged the mill located next to the rail station. The mill, still in the Rogers family, continues to mix and sell feed and the train station is a part of that property. The years and economic challenges were not kind to the W&OD, and in response to varying fortunes, it discontinued passenger service on April 23, 1941. With the gasoline shortage caused by World War II, emergency service began again in March 1943 but ended finally in 1946. Passenger service was completely abandoned on May 31, 1951.

Three weekly newspapers were published in Hamilton. The first, The Loudoun Enterprise, began on January 31, 1871. In 1890 The Loudoun Telephone was published, giving Hamilton its second newspaper which for some time was the only Republican newspaper in Northern Virginia. The Weekly Enterprise, a Democratic paper, began in 1890. Sometime between 1905 and 1909, the name of the paper would become simply The Enterprise and was moved to Purcellville in the early 1920s.

Town Sign

Masonic Hall

Due to the type of construction, heating and cooking practices of the late 19th century, fire was a very real concern. On March 22, 1926, an unimaginable disaster occurred. A fire had started in the basement of a clothing store, which showed evidence of having been robbed, and was making rapid headway both east and west. The fire didn't cross the street, but spread to adjoining buildings in both directions. The fire lasted until late afternoon. When it was over, six businesses, including the Post Office, and four homes had been lost. Only four of the original businesses were re-established and only one home rebuilt.

In 1860 the Village's population was but 148 people. By 1890 the Town's population had grown to more than 400. The population of Hamilton, inside the town limits, as of 2009, reached 797, up from 562 in 2000. In the early 20th century, Hamilton was a major centre of economic and cultural activity. Tourists arrived by train. The Town's main street was lined with a milliner's shop, clothing stores, a butcher, a drug store, a creamery, places of worship, and of course, graceful, comfortable boarding houses and private homes. Dentists and doctors were readily available, and the Town even had two undertakers. Newspapers kept visitor and resident alike informed. Modern communications arrived in Hamilton in 1886 when the Hamilton Telephone Company was allowed to erect the necessary poles for telephones.

Today, Hamilton is primarily a residential community. Some believe the Town's decline in economic activity began with the devastating fire of March 1926. Others believe it was the advent of the automobile which afforded increased mobility and less reliance on the limitations of the railroad. Whatever the root cause, Hamilton has succeeded in keeping its rich cultural and historical heritage safe by resisting the lure of greater prosperity by expansion of its corporate boundaries. Much of the surrounding farm land has been bought by developers and large, single-family, custom-built homes have been built on three acre lots. While the population has continued to grow, both inside and outside the Town's corporate boundaries, much of that population lives outside the boundaries of the incorporated Town.

Hamilton is an historic small town in a rural setting, committed to preserving its character and respecting its natural resources. About 70 buildings, primarily along Hamilton's main street, are more than 100 years old. Its properties are dotted with mature trees, contributing to the beauty of the Town.

Hamilton's traditions help maintain its hometown feel. Residents celebrate 'Hamilton Day' every spring with a parade through the centre of town, followed by barbecues, park festivities, home tours, and children's activities. In 1945 the tradition of presenting a sleek, hand-turned, silver-tipped cane to Hamilton's oldest male resident began and continues today. Each Christmas the Town's living Christmas Tree, at the entrance to the park, is lit in early December. On Christmas Eve the entire length of Hamilton's main street is lined with luminaries assembled and distributed by volunteers who reside in and around the Town. At dusk each home owner lights the luminary in front of their home. The Town and residents of nearby communities value the Hamilton Community Park. Built in 1986 the park was the vision of a former Mayor, Ruth Tillett. The park served as a playground until it was closed for safety reasons in 1999. The community rallied and created a new playground now enjoyed by children of all ages.

Hamilton remains a safe and happy place to live and to raise a family.

Text and Photographs – Donna Norton

Bank in Hamilton City, Virginia.

Hamilton Post Office and Sundry Store

HAMILTON CITY , GREENWOOD COUNTY, KANSAS, 1880

Hamilton is a city in Greenwood County, Kansas. As of the 2010 census, the city population was 268. The city was named in honour of Alexander Hamilton. The city should not be confused with Hamilton County.

Although Hamilton received its designation as a town in 1880, it was actually settled between Willow and Slate Creeks in 1870. It was originally planned to be called Fullerton, but another town had already claimed that name. So in honour of Alexander Hamilton, the town of Hamilton, Kansas was founded.

At that time, Hamilton was the closest city to the centre of the county. In the early years, cattle were shipped in and out of Hamilton by railroad. The Hamilton stockyard was the largest line from Emporia to Howard City and it had the ability to handle 800 head of cattle per shipment. Hamilton's economy is still rooted in agriculture and oil.

Hamilton City Hall and Fire Station
Photographs supplied by Greenwood County Tourism

HAMILTON, PEMBINA COUNTY, NORTH DAKOTA, 1882

Hamilton, North Dakota is located in Eastern Pembina County. The city is located along North Dakota Highway 5, about 10 miles west of Interstate 29. It was founded in 1882. Many residents of the community have Norwegian and German ancestry.

According to the 2010 U.S. Census, 61 people lived in Hamilton.

Hamilton is surrounded by the rich soil of the Red River Valley and because of this the community has always been agriculturally-based. Hamilton is best known for housing the Pembina County Fair, "The Biggest Little Fair in North Dakota."

On September 24, 1894, the Pembina County Fair Association was reorganized. The original name had been Pembina County Annual Fair and Exchange Association. In 1894 the fair was held on October 2nd and 3rd at Hamilton, North Dakota.

The Pembina County Fair is the oldest continuous running fair in North Dakota.

Hamilton has limited services available. It does offer a bank and a bar!

Above Left: Hamilton Post Office and Café. Photograph by Matchbox ND
Above Centre: Entrance Gates to Pembina County Fair in Hamilton, North Dakota
Above Right: United Methodist Church (Centre for Heritage)

HAMILTON, MARION COUNTY, ALABAMA, 1883

Hamilton is located in the beautiful hills of Northwest Alabama, 100 miles northwest of Birmingham, Alabama and 50 miles east of Tupelo, Mississippi.

Hamilton is situated almost in the centre of Marion County. The roots of the county go back to the early history of the State of Alabama. Marion County takes its name from the Revolutionary War Hero Frances Marion, and was created as the largest Alabama territorial county in 1818. At this time the county stretched deep into what is now South Alabama and Mississippi. Settlers from Tennessee, Kentucky, Georgia, and the Carolinas came here to settle what was then known as the Mid-Western Frontier. Hamilton, in its early history was first known as Toll Gate, named for a toll-gate on the old Military Road.

Hamilton spans the historic route known as "Military Road", which was carved out of the wilderness by volunteer soldiers from Tennessee returning north to their homes from victory over the British at New Orleans in 1815. The army of General Andrew Jackson - who ordered the development of the road as a short cut between New Orleans and Nashville - camped at Military Ford, three miles south of Hamilton, as they ventured homeward. The construction of a bike and hiking trail is underway to commemorate the time-honoured road's place in United States history.

The Pikeville area - located just south of Hamilton - served as the county seat for several years until Captain A.J. Hamilton offered to donate 40 acres of his land in Toll Gate to the community. In 1883, the Toll Gate donation from him was accepted following a referendum, and the name of the community was officially changed to Hamilton in his honour. His family home and grave-site are still preserved today.

From a few dozen families and settlers in the 1880s, Hamilton grew rapidly. The first school was established in 1884, and in 1891 evolved into a high school.

Toll Gate and Military Road Indian history and roots are deeply established here. The Chickasaw Tribe hunted here and provided corn to the newly arrived immigrants. One of the upcoming restorative efforts that the City of Hamilton has underway is to re-establish the presence of the Indian burial grounds and mounds that still remain within Hamilton along the banks of the Buttahatchee River.

Above Left: Old Splendour in Hamilton. Photograph by Lee Brown
Above Right: County Courthouse in Hamilton. Photograph by Ben Tate
Centre: Town Sign
Below: Country Lane outside Hamilton. Photograph by Lee Brown

HAMILTON, MOFFAT COUNTY, COLORADO, 1888

As Henry and Mary Hamilton raised their nine children on a farm in DeKalb County, Missouri, they were fulfilling a dream of pursuing an agricultural lifestyle. A former shoemaker, Henry found that farming in the post American Civil War era could be quite profitable. Their hard work paid off well and their dreams came true.

Their oldest son, Riley, helped to work the family farm until 1881 at the age of 19, when the young man decided to make his own way in Colorado. Like so many others before – and after him – he first landed in the mines near Breckenridge. It didn't take long before he realized that working underground wasn't as fulfilling for him as working on top of and in the soil.

Hamilton spent some time working on a ranch in South Park before heading north to Fort Collins where he farmed for two years. His brother Tom joined him in Colorado and in the summer of 1885 the young men made their way to Routt County where there were few people, but many opportunities.

The brothers took up a pre-emption and a timber claim totalling 320 acres in the Williams Fork (Moore Rapids) and began to build their futures. They later added more land to their claim with 200 acres under cultivation.

When the men arrived at Williams Fork, after travelling hundreds of miles through unclaimed lands, they found another early settler squatting at the place they thought to take for their own. There wasn't a problem however, because Thomas Iles decided to move farther west. He settled on a piece of land that would make history in the development of Northwest Colorado and the energy industry when massive amounts of oil and gas were discovered on his chosen homestead. When the Hamiltons took up their homestead, they had no close neighbours, roads or other amenities. They worked hard to improve their land as did the neighbours who gradually settled in the area.

The brothers eventually split their holdings, with Tom taking the northernmost section, including an area where the roads on the Williams Fork and Morapos Creek met.

In 1896 a post office was established in Hamilton with Tom's father-in-law, J.B. Johnston, serving as postmaster. A small store followed a few years later and the little community continued to grow. Riley's homestead soon became the site for the

mail and stage stop for travellers between Craig, 18 miles to the north and Meeker, 32 miles to the south.

It was a close-knit community made up of strong people who cared about each other as well as their own families. When the community school burned to the ground in 1922, they were quick to rebuild. The three-roomed building was valued at $400 and the school furniture at $300. In addition all the pupils lost their school books.

Nearly half a century after the Hamilton brothers settled on the Williams Fork, the first energy boom hit Northwest Colorado when the Hamilton oil dome was drilled by the Texas Company. That well was the first of many that would change the course of the area and the State of Colorado. The Discovery well came in at 5,000 barrels of high quality oil a day and the race was on.

By 1924 Hamilton, once the 'halfway house' for cowpunchers and freighters, had a figurative shot in the arm.

This changed the Tom Hamilton ranch into a booming little town, with the sound of carpenters' hammers drowning out the coyote's wails. It is conservatively estimated that Hamilton then had a population of some two hundred, where six months earlier the citizens could be counted on the fingers of one hand.

The little town was only a mile from the Discovery well and just a few more miles from the massive oil field that was being opened.

Tom Hamilton partnered with J. E. Frost, an experienced town site planner. The men laid out 2,000 lots on the 160 acre Hamilton homestead and built up a real trading point. Streets were laid out and named, a park was planned in the beautiful trees along the river. The town adjoins the Hamilton oil dome and is the junction of two pipe lines.

Boarding houses, shops and restaurants quickly rose from the land as people rushed to get their share of the boom. The Otten store and the Hamilton's lunch room were the first two businesses to serve the growing population but they were joined by new businesses daily as the swelling population packed into the area.

In 1924 it was one of the most thickly populated spots in Moffat County. Scores of tents and temporary shelters housed the majority of Hamilton's population and space on which to pitch a tent was at a premium

The quick construction served a purpose, but it also lent itself to quick destruction. In the few years following the initial building frenzy, several of the structures fell to fires. In 1943 the post office and main store were levelled in a fast-moving fire. In typical fashion though, the residents of Hamilton came together and rebuilt.

Little remains today of the bustling little oil town of the 1920s, but the people of Hamilton continue to collect their mail at their post office and gather regularly at the community building. There are approximately 40 people residing in this area today, many who are the third or fourth generation living on their land. The core of the community remains and as new residents move into the area, they discover a little gem along the Williams Fork.

Located in remote and hilly country, the small community continues in its agricultural roots, with small and large ranch tracts that sustain mostly cattle and sheep operations, while Hamilton is now a hub for new endeavours in oil and gas exploration.

Hamilton Community Centre and Post Office at elevation of 6240 feet
Text - Mary Pat Dunn
Photographs by Melody Villard

HAMILTON CROSSROADS, PIKE COUNTY, ALABAMA, 1888

The year was 1888 and gunfire had not been silenced for long from the American Civil War that ripped the country apart.

The community of Hamilton Crossroads sprung up soon after the American Civil War. It was named after Mr Lum Hamilton, who ran the local store in the community.

In 1888, a man by the name of Dr S.I.S. Cawthon, made his first of several visits to the crossroads. Dr Cawthon was a doctor by profession prior to his conversion to Christ; however, he gave that up to preach the simple gospel of Jesus Christ. Dr Cawthon approached Mr Hamilton with the interest of starting a congregation in the community.

His efforts aroused the interests of several women and men who built a brush arbour for shade as Dr Cawthon preached. Soon after, the Pea River waters would be used to baptize several men and women of the community. The local school house opened its doors to these men and women and soon the church numbered 103. For several years the young congregation held their worship services at the local school houses. However, around 1902, opposition arose over the use of public facilities for religious services. A small vacant lot was found north of the Carter Brother's Manufacturing Company and a small building erected to house the Christian family. Ten years later, 1912, a need for a new building arose and Mr Sam Clark was hired to oversee the construction of the building. This building still stands today and holds many wonderful memories for a large number of the members. For 50 years this building served as the location for meetings of the membership of Hamilton Crossroads. In September of 1962, the decision was made to purchase 2 acres of land from Robert and Neil McClendon for the purpose of erecting a new building. Once again the church had outgrown the current facilities. On January 7th, 1962 the new building was dedicated and ever since has served the current membership.

Over the years, the church at Hamilton Crossroads has experienced steady numerical and spiritual growth. Several men over the years have served the church as elders.

Through the years the church at Hamilton Crossroads has had an amazing impact on the surrounding communities.

HAMILTON, SKAGIT COUNTY, WASHINGTON, 1891

Hamilton is a town in Skagit County, Washington. The population was 301 at the 2010 census.

Hamilton was first settled in 1877 by William Hamilton, and was later named for him when Hamilton was officially incorporated on March 19, 1891.

HAMILTON, RAVALLI COUNTY, MONTANA, 1894

Hamilton, Montana is the Ravalli County seat of Government and the largest town in the Bitterroot Valley. This expansive, big sky, valley contains the Bitterroot River which runs south from the border of Idaho northward to Missoula where it joins the Clark River.

Hamilton was founded by copper king Marcus Daly in the late 19th century. It was incorporated in 1894 and named for James W. Hamilton, an employee of Daly who platted the town along the route of the Northern Pacific Railroad in 1890. Daly is said to have wanted to begin business in the then county seat of Grantsdale, but was denied the opportunity. He supposedly founded Hamilton out of his own pocket as a reaction to being rebuffed at Grantsdale. Marcus Daly was one of Montana's colourful "Copper Kings." He was an Irish immigrant who made his fortune in the mines of Butte and founded the Anaconda Mining Company and established the town of Anaconda. Daly came to the Bitterroot Valley in search of timber for his mines - and this he found in abundance. He built a mill to process the timber and formed a company town around the mill for the workers. He built a beautiful summer home in the valley in 1887 and accumulated large tracts of land for his hobby of breeding and racing thoroughbred horses. This large ranch was named the Bitter Root Stock Farm.

By the time Daly died in 1900, Hamilton was the commercial centre of the Bitterroot Valley and the seat of Ravalli County.

The years from 1907 to 1911 in the Bitterroot Valley were termed the "Apple Boom." Many other towns in the west had their boom days fuelled by mining discoveries, but Hamilton received its heritage from the enthusiasm of slick salesmen who took advantage of an extensive irrigation network conceived by Marcus Daly. Enticed by the promise of fertile land and a good climate for growing fruit trees, many unsuspecting farmers came to the valley to give it a go. From 1907 to 1911 the town's population jumped from 1,800 to 3,000.

By 1915 all the easily accessible timber had been cut from the valley and The Anaconda Copper Mining Company Mill closed. Two years after that the financial problems of the irrigation ditch builders reached a head and the Apple Boom went bust. Many orchard farmers became disillusioned and moved away.

Two Views of Tammany Hall – A famous Hamilton landmark

The local economy remained shaky until 1927 when the Rocky Mountain Laboratory was established to research the cause of Rocky Mountain Spotted Fever. Contrary to other parts of the nation, Hamilton enjoyed considerable growth during the depression years of the thirties until World War II.

Hamilton and Ravalli County are currently experiencing another economic boom. The valley has been discovered as an outdoor paradise by urban professionals escaping the rat race. The valley currently has a population of over 35,000.

In the summer of 2000, Hamilton made international headlines when forest fires throughout the Bitterroot Valley filled the area with smoke and prompted the evacuation of many residents. President Clinton declared a state of emergency in the area and dispatched National Guardsmen to assist with fighting the fires.

The Bitterroot Valley is named after the "bitterroot", which is now Montana's state flower and used to be an important food source for the Indian tribes in the valley. Though this plant is quite bitter in its raw form, it commanded a high price in trading and was a fine meal when boiled and mixed with meat or berries. Pulverized and seasoned with deer fat and moss, the cooked root could be moulded into patties and carried on hunting expeditions or war parties.

The Bitterroot Valley is framed to the west by the Bitterroot Mountains, and to the east by the Sapphires. The Bitterroot River starts just below the Continental Divide near Lost Trail Pass on the Idaho/Montana border which is 7,014 feet in elevation and ends near Missoula at an elevation of 3,210 feet. Hamilton holds a central position in the valley at about 3,500 feet above sea level and enjoys a temperate climate which is often referred to as the "Banana Belt" of Montana.

The Bitterroot Valley is a haven for outdoor enthusiasts providing a great richness of wildlife and outdoor opportunities. This valley borders the two largest Federal wilderness areas in the US: the Selway-Bitterroot Wilderness and the Anaconda-Pintler Wilderness. Hunting and fishing is abundant. Fresh air, pleasant climate and beautiful scenery make this a backpacker's paradise. Hundreds of rafters enjoy the Bitterroot River in the summer. Cross country and downhill skiing are popular activities in the winter.

Above Right: Bitterroot Autumn
Below Right: The fires of 2000 seen from Main Street, Hamilton

The Bitterroot Valley. Photographs by R.Landry

Inuit preparing a seal in Hamilton, Alaska. Photograph by Thomas Bruns

Kotlik post Office, the closest to Hamilton. Photograph by Huskydog

HAMILTON, ALASKA, 1897

The site is located on the right bank of Apoon Pass, southwest of Kotlik, in the Yukon Delta. The community is located in the Bethel Recording District. The area encompasses 5 square miles of land.

The village was first reported in 1844 by Lt. L.A. Zagoskin of the Russian Navy as the Inuit village or camp "Aunguamut." In 1897, the North American Transportation & Trading Company established a supply post and riverboat landing here. The village was named after Charles H. Hamilton, assistant manager of the company, who also had a Yukon River Steamboat named after him. It has also been known as Fort Hamilton and Old Hamilton.

Cactus and old house in Hamilton. Photograph by Maria

HAMILTON CITY, GLENN COUNTY, CALIFORNIA, 1905

Hamilton City was named after James G. Hamilton who with the help of his brother Charles and his son Ernest Clydesdale Hamilton, founded the town in 1905-06. First known as just "Hamilton," it was changed at the request of the U.S. Post Office Department because there was another "Hamilton" just across the Sacramento River in neighbouring Butte County. The U.S .Post Office in Hamilton City was established on May 26, 1906 with Edwin E. Parker as postmaster.

Hamilton City was established by incorporating the early settlements of St. John and Monroeville in 1905. James G.Hamilton was an instrumental figure in bringing the sugar beet industry to the region by opening the Alta California Beet Sugar Company factory in Hamilton City in 1906. This plant was later owned by the Sacramento Valley Sugar Company [1908], Holly Sugar Company [1936], and Imperial Holly Sugar Company [1988], and helped to organise the construction of the Colusa & Hamilton Railway to the sugar factory. The railroad was deeded to the Southern Pacific Railroad

Company in 1917. The railroad to the sugar factory still exists but the factory has been closed since June 1996. Hamilton City currently has a population of around 1,800 and is not an incorporated city.

James G. Hamilton was a New York banker and stock broker when he became interested in making sugar from sugar beets. With other investors, they formed a sugar beet company and established factories in Nebraska (1890) and southern California.

The Oxnard Construction Company was organized to "devote itself to developing the sugar (beet) growing and manufacturing industry in this country." The officers of the company were Henry T. Oxnard, President; James G. Hamilton, Vice President; W. Bayard Cutting, Treasurer; S.D. Scheuck, Secretary; and Wilhelm Baur, Chief Executive Officer. Main office was in New York City, New York. "Mr Hamilton has been secretary of various sugar factories since they have been in existence." In 1901, James G. Hamilton was the Secretary of the American Beet Sugar Manufacturers' Association.

James G. and son Ernest C. Hamilton came to Glenn County, California in their search for new places to grow sugar beets and to build sugar factories. Machinery and electric water pumps from the east were intended for the Hamilton City factory but were destroyed in the San Francisco earthquake and fire of April 18, 1906. Ernest Clydesdale Hamilton is listed in the Glenn County Great Register, Hamilton Precinct, for 1906 as being 32 years of age and listed as a "Sugarmaker."

James G. Hamilton is listed in the 1910 U.S. Census living in New York City and married to wife Virginia Cuthbert Hamilton for 40 years. The 1920 U.S .Census has James and Virginia Hamilton living in Long Beach, Los Angeles County, California. James G. Hamilton was born circa 1848 in New York State with his father born in Nova Scotia, Canada and his mother born in Massachusetts. James and Virginia were the parents of at least four children—Lillian, Ernest, Grace, and Emmett.

Hamilton and his company lost their money when the factory came on hard times and eventually closed. James G. and Virginia Hamilton moved from New York to Long Beach, California in 1918 and James died in February 1926 (age 78) and Mrs. Hamilton passed away in March 1934.

Landmark grain elevators are still visible from all over town. "La Palmas" (Palm Drive) is also a well known landmark 2.1 miles in length.

Above: Grain Elevators. Photograph by Kimberlee Wheeler
Above Right: Las Palmas. Photograph by Andy Tomaselli
Below Right: Almonds growing in Hamilton, Glenn County.
Photograph by Kimberlee Wheeler
Text - Gene H. Russell, Ed.D.

Hamilton Dome today

HAMILTON DOME, HOT SPRINGS COUNTY, WYOMING, 1918

In 1918, Richard Dean Berry and his family claimed land and discovered what is now known as Hamilton Dome. In order for Richard to turn his claim into his homestead, he had to have a survey done of the land he had claimed. Richard did not have the money to pay for several people to come and survey his land, so he paid for a survey and he assisted the surveyor. While doing the survey, Richard immediately recognized the land as being a perfect oil structure. A perfect oil structure is a geological dome. How they decided this in the older days was by determining how the land slopes in all directions from a central point, forming what looks like a dome. Richard consulted with Dr A.G. Hamilton who was the family doctor and a good friend to him. Dr Hamilton financially assisted Richard at the start, and therefore Richard Berry named his claim Hamilton Dome.

Text and Photograph by Shyla Buckner

HAMILTON LAKE, GARLAND COUNTY, ARKANSAS, USA, 1932

The area of the Ouachita River near Hot Springs and Malvern, Arkansas was a virtual wilderness in the 1920s when Harvey Couch, the founder of Arkansas Power and Light Company, now known as Entergy, began to investigate his dream of building hydro-electric dams on the Ouachita River as part of his programme of "Helping Build Arkansas" by bringing new industry and jobs to the state.

In 1932 Carpenter Dam was constructed at the headwater above Lake Catherine. It was named after Flave Carpenter, the pioneer peace officer who first discovered the dam site while searching for outlaws along the river, who recommended it to Couch. The resulting lake was 18 ½ miles long and covered 7,200 acres. Couch named it Lake Hamilton in honour of his faithful attorney, C. Hamilton Moses, who assumed the Presidency of AP&L after Couch's death in 1941.

Now, in addition to being a magnet for fishermen and water sports enthusiasts, the lakes region and the community of Hamilton Lake are a popular base camp for day hikes and overnight backpack trips into the rugged Ouachita Mountains and for nature study and wildlife photography. The region offers opportunities for outdoor recreation in all its many forms.

If you want a quiet walk in undisturbed woodlands, an adventurous family can sample its own "deserted island" in Lake Hamilton by exploring Electric Island. This 118 acre island was donated by Entergy to the Arkansas Nature Conservancy in 1984 and is leased to the Arkansas Game and Fish Commission for non-game wildlife management. It is dominated by tall pines and shady groves and is frequented by bald eagles during the winter season. It is located due north of the Arkansas Game and Fish Commission hatchery.

There are free swimming areas on Lake Hamilton in addition to privately owned facilities which charge a user's fee. Boating is one of the most popular sports on the lakes, and there are numerous boat launching ramps. In addition, various concessioners rent boats and motors to the public.

Water-skiers delight in the more than 14 square miles of surface area available on Lake Hamilton and Lake Catherine and the many extended coves which offer a calm surface. Canoeing, kayaking and paddle boating are also popular on the lakes, and various types of small craft can be rented.

Lake Hamilton, the surrounding Diamond Lakes Region, and Hot Springs National Park have long been famous for their geothermal hot mineral waters. The Park's historic "Bathhouse Row" and the downtown Hot Springs business district are just a short distance from Lake Hamilton. Oaklawn Park remains one of the most popular horse racing and gaming venues in the south. Luxury resorts and marinas now blend into the pine-shrouded shoreline of Lake Catherine and Lake Hamilton.

Text and Photographs – Hot Springs Visitor Service

C HAMILTON MOSES (1888 – 1966)

Colter Hamilton Moses served as secretary to governors George W. Donaghey, George W. Hays, and Charles Hillman Brough prior to becoming general counsel, president, and chairman of the board of Arkansas Power and Light (AP&L). Well known as an eloquent speaker, Moses represented the Governor's Office in an entourage that travelled around the country promoting Arkansas; however, his greatest contribution to Arkansas resulted in the state moving from an agricultural economy to an industrial one during the post–World War II years. Although the state's economy grew monumentally because of Moses' efforts, he credited the people of Arkansas for the success of his "Arkansas Plan."

C. Hamilton (Ham) Moses, the eldest of Angelus Gaston, "A. G.", Moses and Mary Eulodia Dunn Moses' three sons, was born on a farm in Hampton on June 28, 1888. His father was a farmer and lumberjack, and his mother taught first grade in Calhoun County schools. As a youth, Moses worked long hours performing farm chores and working in south Arkansas' logging camps. After attending Hampton public schools, Moses graduated from Ouachita College (now Ouachita Baptist University) in 1908, where he specialized in debate and public speaking; from Tulane University in 1910 with a master's degree in Southern history; and from the University of Arkansas Law Department in Little Rock in 1911. He married Lena Goodwin of El Dorado in September 1912, and they had three daughters and one son.

While Moses attended law school in Little Rock, he worked briefly in the Arkansas Department of Education prior to becoming Governor Donaghey's secretary. When Donaghey left office, Moses relocated to Monticello and became the law partner of prosecuting attorney Bob Wilson. He maintained a law office in Monticello while serving as secretary to Governor Hays and Governor Brough. Moses and T. Dwight Crawford co-authored the Moses and Crawford Digest of Statutes in Arkansas, which was published in 1921. In 1919, Moses opened a law office in Little Rock and became general counsel to all of Harvey Couch's business enterprises, including AP&L. In 1925, Moses joined U.S. Senator Joe T. Robinson and Joe House to form the law firm of Robinson, House, and Moses. After Couch's death in 1941, Moses became president of AP&L.

During World War II, private power companies profited greatly as they operated at full capacity to meet war production demands; however, decreased power loads after the war created financial difficulties for utility companies, which eventually led to an intense struggle between public and private power entities in the 1940s. To increase public demand for electricity, Moses initiated his "Arkansas Plan," designed to encourage community leaders to utilize local residents, resources, capital, and labour to strengthen their communities and attract business and industry into the state. The University of Arkansas in Fayetteville, state organizations, and private corporations supported his efforts and organized to form the Arkansas Economic Council in December 1944.

Moses, Arkansas's business cheerleader, visited many Arkansas communities and motivated Arkansans to demonstrate civic pride in their towns by making notable improvements to attract new industry. As a result, local residents enhanced their communities by paving city streets, whitewashing storefronts, landscaping public property, and developing recreational programmes. They also built new houses, churches, hospitals, and schools, which attracted more industry to the state. Moses then travelled around the country preaching "the gospel of Arkansas" to draw corporate attention to the state. Within ten years, the state reaped bountiful harvests as new industry created 36,000 jobs with an annual payroll of $200 million, and Arkansas' per capita income increased 225 per cent; bank deposits rose 281 per cent; and manufacturing volume soared 451 per cent.

Moses retired as president of AP&L in 1952 but remained Chairman of the Board until 1955. He then formed the Little Rock law firm of Moses, McClellan, Arnold, Owen, and McDermott. Before his death, several business groups honoured Moses for his efforts. He was named Arkansas' Outstanding Citizen (1947), Arkansas Man of the Year (1948), and Man of the South (1950), and he received the Freedoms Foundation medal (1950). Harvey Couch honoured Moses by naming Lake Hamilton for him. In December 1953, Reader's Digest journalist William Hard aptly paid tribute to Moses by stating, "What a diplomat! What a businessman! What a promoter of social service! What a resister of socialization! What a fighter! What a Rebel!"

He died in 1966.

Photograph courtesy of Encyclopaedia of Arkansas

HAMILTON (FIELD), MARIN COUNTY, CALIFORNIA, 1932

Hamilton Air Force Base was a United States Air Force base located along the western shore of San Pablo Bay, south of Novato, California.

What would eventually become Hamilton Air Force Base has its origins in the late 1920s, when the airfield was first established. Known at first unofficially as the Marin County Air Field, as Marin Airfield, as Marin Meadows Air Field, and as the Army Air Base at Marin Meadows, it was officially termed from 1929 until 1932 the "Air Corps Station, San Rafael." Then, with formal development beginning, it was named Hamilton Army Air Field on July 12, 1932.

Hamilton Airfield was named for First Lieutenant Lloyd Andrews Hamilton of the 17th Aero Squadron.

During World War II, Hamilton was an important West Coast air training facility. Its mission was that of an initial training base for newly-formed fighter groups. The airfield was rapidly expanded to a wartime status, with construction of additional barracks, mess halls, administration buildings, warehouses, Link trainer buildings, schools, hospital and other structures.

The Air Force curtailed its activities on the base after October 1, 1973 when the 452d was relieved of host base responsibility, with most of the base being transferred to the U.S. Army as Hamilton Army Airfield. The Pacific Strike Team of the U.S. Coast Guard occupied two of the historic hangars. The housing was transferred to the U.S. Navy and a 411 acre parcel of the base was transferred to the General Services Administration (GSA) for public sale.

Decades of work have transformed the former Air Force base into a delightful community.

Today, more than 30 years since the last jet fighter blasted off a nearby runway, Hamilton's hangars are sleek office buildings. As for those miles of runways, they're soon to be flooded and turned into permanent wetlands—stopping places for squadrons of waterfowl navigating the Pacific Flyway.

Hamilton, located within the city of Novato, has been hailed as one of the finest military

Aerial View of the old Hamilton Field Air Force Base

base conversions in the country. The 2,200 acres adjacent to the former hangars and runways were once the site of base housing, officers' clubs, recreation halls and military administrative buildings. Now they are crossed by meandering streets lined uniformly with young-growth trees and blocks of tidy homes occupied by a mix of young and old, wealthy and working class.

1ST LIEUTENANT LLOYD ANDREWS HAMILTON, (1894 – 1918)

Plaque in memory of Lloyd Andrews Hamilton

First Lieutenant Lloyd Andrews Hamilton was a World War I flying ace credited with ten aerial victories. During five months of 1918 he became an ace with the Royal Flying Corps. Lloyd Andrews Hamilton was born in Troy, New York, the only child of a Methodist minister. When America entered World War I, he enlisted in the USAS on 28 April and in May he reported to Plattsburgh, New York, for officer training. Hamilton then went to England and joined the RFC. Hamilton was awarded the DFC and then the DSC for heroism at Varssonaore, Belgium, in leading a low level bombing attack on a German aerodrome 30 miles behind enemy lines on August 13, 1918. Thirteen days later Hamilton died in action near Lagnicourt, France.

Other Hamiltons in the USA

HAMILTON CORNER, MARICOPA COUNTY, ARIZONA

Hamilton High School at Hamilton Corner

Hamilton High School's Stadium

Hamilton Library
Photographys by Al Macbeane

Hamilton Corner is a suburb of Chandler in Maricopa County, Arizona.

HAMILTON, LONOKE COUNTY, ARKANSAS

The Township of Hamilton is one of twenty-nine townships in Lonoke County, Arkansas. As of the 2000 census, its total population was 175. It is named after Hamilton Reynolds, a local surveyor.

HAMILTON BRANCH, PLUMAS COUNTY, CALIFORNIA

A community of 587 on the banks of Lake Almanor.

Lake Almanor at dusk. Photograph by stett3

Lassen Peak from Hamilton Branch. Photograph by Dana Westendarp

HAMILTON, CHAFFEE COUNTY, COLORADO

Hamilton was founded after prospectors from Leadville camped out in Clear Creek Canyon and their burros wandered down to the creek. The next day the prospectors found their animals and also found good float in the creek. Many towns sprang up along the creek including Hamilton. Hamilton was mainly a company mining camp of the Hamilton Mining and Tunnel Company. It consisted of only four or five log structures, and the operation closed down in 1905. It is the most remote mining camp of Clear Creek Canyon.

The ghost town of Hamilton can be accessed only on foot - it is in a wilderness area and vehicles are prohibited. If you keep going past the banker mine on the 4x4 road, you'll come to the U.S. Forest gate and have about an hour and a half hike to the ghost town of Hamilton (or what's left of it). There is only about half of the mining camp office composed of maybe 8 or 9 logs and it sits across the creek where you really can't get to it!

HAMILTON PARK, NEW CASTLE COUNTY, DELAWARE

Hamilton Park is a small suburb of Wilmington, Delaware.

HAMILTON LAKE, POLK COUNTY, FLORIDA

Hamilton Lake is a town with a population of around 1,400.

Hamilton Lake

HAMILTON CORNER, PAYETTE COUNTY, IDAHO

A populated place.

HAMILTON TOWNSHIP, LEE COUNTY, ILLINOIS

Hamilton has a population of 236.

HAMILTON, DELAWARE COUNTY, INDIANA

Hamilton Township is one of twelve townships in Delaware County, Indiana. As of the 2000 census, its population was 7,163.

HAMILTON, JACKSON COUNTY, INDIANA

Hamilton Township is one of twelve townships in Jackson County, Indiana. As of the 2000 census, its population was 1,615.

HAMILTON, MADISON COUNTY, INDIANA

Hamilton is an unincorporated town in Jackson Township, Madison County.

HAMILTON TOWNSHIP, SULLIVAN COUNTY, INDIANA

Hamilton Township is one of nine townships in Sullivan County, Indiana. Its population is around 7,500. Sullivan, the County seat, is situated in Hamilton Township.

Court Street, Sullivan, Hamilton Township. Photograph by Nyttend

Sullivan County Courthouse. Photograph by Donna Adams

Sullivan County Lake and Park has lots to offer with its 461 acre lake, constructed in 1968 for the purpose of flood control and conservation, swimming, boating and fishing. The lake is well stocked with crappie and hybrid saugeye, as well as bass, bluegill and channel catfish. Water skiing is also very popular on Lake Sullivan. The park area provides various outdoor facilities including a campground, 9 hole golf course and playground. Sullivan County Airport is a county-owned public-use airport located 6 kilometres northwest of the central business district of Sullivan. The Airport covers an area of 108 acres and it has one asphalt paved runway.

Sullivan Lake. Photograph by Bellbucksnbeards

HAMILTON, MARION COUNTY, IOWA

A small place with a population of 144.

HAMILTON, WEST FELICIANA PARISH, LOUISIANA

Listed as a populated place there were Hamilton families, who were slave owners, in West Feliciana in the early 1800s.

HAMILTON, BALTIMORE, MARYLAND

The neighbourhood was originally farmland along the Harford Road corridor, which at the time was a major arterial route out of Baltimore City into the much more rural Harford County. The area began to be developed in the late 1910s and early 1920s and, for some areas, into the 1950s. Architecturally, most of the homes are similar to each other, and are larger, 1920s and 1930s era houses. There are small pockets of the famous brick-faced Baltimore rowhouses scattered throughout the area, especially along Harford Road south of Echodale Avenue.

Hamilton evolved into a mixed-race, middle class suburb in the 1970s and 1980s. With the shutting of the Arcade Theatre in the early 1980s, a large, community-oriented plaza and movie house was suddenly vacant, and urban blight began to creep into the commercial and cultural centre of Hamilton.

Beginning in the early 2000s, the Harford Road corridor has seen increased urban development with award winning restaurants coming into the area. Two art galleries and the Hamilton Arts Collective can also be found along the stretch of Harford Road that runs through Hamilton.

Harford Road in the Hamilton Suburb of Baltimore

HAMILTON PARK, WASHINGTON COUNTY, MARYLAND

A suburb of Hagerstown, Maryland.

HAMILTON, WORCESTER COUNTY, MASSACHUSETTS

A small suburb of Worcester.

Apple Orchard in Winter, Hamilton, Clare County. Photograph by Tony Stackpole

HAMILTON TOWNSHIP, CLARE COUNTY, MICHIGAN

Hamilton Township is a civil township of Clare County in the state of Michigan. As of the 2000 census, the township population was 1,988.

HAMILTON TOWNSHIP, GRATIOT COUNTY, MICHIGAN

Hamilton Township is a civil township of Gratiot County in the state of Michigan. As of the 2000 census, the township population was 491.

HAMILTON, VAN BUREN COUNTY, MICHIGAN

Hamilton Township is a civil township of Van Buren County in the state of Michigan. As of the 2000 census, the township population was 1,797. The township is mostly agricultural with no towns. There are some private campgrounds and cottages at Lake-of-the-Woods.

Sunrise at Lake-of-the –Woods, Hamilton, Van Buren County. Photograph by M Cajas

HAMILTON, FILLMORE COUNTY, MINNESOTA

Hamilton is a small place, 20 miles south of Rochester.

HAMILTON, BENTON COUNTY, MISSISSIPPI

Hamilton is a small place, 70 miles east of Memphis.

HAMILTON, MONROE COUNTY, MISSISSIPPI

Hamilton is an unincorporated community in Monroe County, Mississippi. It was the original county seat until Monroe County was split with the formation of Lowndes County to the south; the county seat of Monroe County was then moved north to Aberdeen.

HAMILTON, HARRISON COUNTY, MISSOURI

Hamilton is a small place about 50 miles north east of Kansas City.

HAMILTON, ST FRANCOIS COUNTY, MISSOURI

A populated place!

HAMILTON, FILLMORE COUNTY, NEBRASKA

Hamilton Township is one of fifteen townships in Fillmore County, Nebraska. The population was 171 at the 2000 census. A 2006 estimate placed the township's population at 161.

GLEN HAMILTON, NYE COUNTY, NEVADA

There was a post office at Glen Hamilton from May 18, 1866 to October 15, 1866. Why, no one has been able to figure out because few people ever lived at Glen Hamilton. It was a small stage stop on the lone to Austin stage run. Today nothing at all remains in the area and the site location is approximate.

FORT HAMILTON DISTRICT, BROOKLYN, NEW YORK

Fort Hamilton is a neighbourhood in the far south-western corner of the New York City borough of Brooklyn. It is located south of, and often considered part of, Bay Ridge. The area stretches from 86th Street as its northern border to 101st Street/the Narrows at the south; it is bounded by New York Bay on the west, and 7th Avenue on the east. The neighbourhood is named for the United States Army installation of the same name which is featured earlier in the book. Fort Hamilton is patrolled by the NYPD's 68thPrecinct.

The Verrazano Bridge at Sunset, taken from the Hamilton Fort district
Photograph by J Mullahy

HAMILTON TOWNSHIP, JACKSON COUNTY, OHIO

Hamilton Township is one of the twelve townships of Jackson County. As of the 2000 census, 513 people lived in the township.

Patriotic Owners in Hamilton. Photograph by alkak1

A rural scene in Hamilton Township, Adams County

HAMILTON TOWNSHIP, ADAMS COUNTY, PENNSYLVANIA

Hamilton Township is a township in Adams County, Pennsylvania. The population was 2,044 at the 2000 census.

Two Mile Run in Hamilton Township, McKean County

HAMILTON, MCKEAN COUNTY, PENNSYLVANIA

As of 2011, Hamilton township's population was 566 people. Olmsted Manor in Ludlow is an historic building within the township.

Olmsted Manor, Hamilton, McKean County. Photograph by John R Plate

HAMILTON, NORTHUMBERLAND COUNTY, PENNSYLVANIA

Hamilton is a sparsely populated outlying suburb of Sunbury.

HAMILTON, PERRY COUNTY, PENNSYLVANIA

Was a settlement based around a bituminous coal mine.

HAMILTON MILL VILLAGE HISTORIC DISTRICT, RHODE ISLAND

Hamilton Mill Village Historic District is on Boston Neck and Martha Roads in North Kingstown, Rhode Island. The district was added to the National Register of Historic Places in 1983.

The Mill Pond. Photograph by Stephanie Parker

WILLIAM HAMILTON TOWNSHIP , HYDE COUNTY, SOUTH DAKOTA

A very sparsely populated township in South Dakota.

HAMILTON, CHARLES MIX COUNTY, SOUTH DAKOTA

Township with a mere 43 people!

HAMILTON, MARSHALL COUNTY, SOUTH DAKOTA

Another remote Township – this time with a population of 28!

Pelicans on Mallard Slough, near Hamilton, Mashall County. Photograph by Ed Jerde

HAMILTON, SULLIVAN COUNTY, TENNESSEE

A hamlet just north of Bluff City.

HAMILTON, DINWIDDIE COUNTY, VIRGINIA

Small unincorporated town south of Richmond.

HAMILTON, WISE COUNTY, VIRGINIA

Appears to be no more than a cemetery!

HAMILTON, CUMBERLAND COUNTY, VIRGINIA

A small unincorporated community.

Above: Fast Food Outlet in Hamilton, Cumberland County.
Below: The disused Hamilton High School. Photographs by R W Dawson

HAMILTON, FAYETTE COUNTY, WEST VIRGINIA

A small hamlet.

MOUNT HAMILTONS

Hamilton Peak is a 13,628 feet mountain peak near Canon City, Colorado.
Mount Hamilton is a 10,699 feet mountain peak near Spring Creek, Nevada.
Hamilton Mesa is a 10,489 feet mountain in New Mexico and has a well known walking trail.
Hamilton Baldy is a 9,488 feet mountain peak near Salida, Colorado.
Hamilton Mesa is a 8,973 feet mountain in Colorado.
Hamilton Butte is a 7,556 feet mountain in Nevada.
Hamilton Mountain is a 7,339 feet mountain in California.
Hamilton Mesa is a 6,398 feet mountain in Arizona.
Hamilton Mesa is a 5,991 feet mountain peak near Towaoc, Colorado.
Hamilton Buttes is a 5,646 feet mountain peak near White Salmon, Washington.
Hamilton Mountain is a 5,325 feet mountain peak near Heppner, Oregon.
Hamilton Mountain is a 5,010 feet mountain in Idaho.
Mount Hamilton is a 3,383 feet mountain in Alaska.
Hamilton Mountain is a 3,215 feet mountain peak near Gloversville, New York.
Hamilton Knob is a 3,038 feet mountain peak near Galax, Virginia.
Hamilton Mountain is a 2,812 feet mountain peak near Coulee Dam, Washington.
Hamilton Mountain is a 2,392 feet mountain peak near Stevenson, Washington.
Hamilton Hill is a 1,765 feet mountain peak near Alfred, New York.
Hamilton Hill is a 1,686 feet mountain in Tennessee.
Hamilton Hill is a 1,132 feet mountain peak near Jonestown, Texas.
Hamilton Knob is a 1,047 feet mountain peak near Buena Vista, Virginia.
Hamilton Mountain is a 1,004 feet mountain peak near Mount Olive, Alabama.
Hamilton Mountain is an 892 feet mountain peak near Varnell, Georgia.
Hamilton Hill is an 804 feet mountain peak near Canton, New York.
Hamilton Hill is a 778 feet mountain peak near Brandenburg, Kentucky.

HAMILTON FALLS

There are Hamilton Falls near Austin, Texas and in Windham County, Vermont.

Hamilton Falls, Vermont. Photograph by Greg Parsons

Canada

HAMILTON TOWNSHIP, NORTHUMBERLAND COUNTY, ONTARIO, 1791

Hamilton Township consists of a cluster of hamlets - Baltimore, Bewdley, Camborne, Cold Springs, Gore's Landing and Harwood - situated in rolling hills between Lake Ontario to the south and Rice Lake to the north. The township, named after Henry Hamilton the first lieutenant-governor of Quebec, was formed shortly after 1791 when Upper Canada (Ontario) was created and divided into Townships. The land was then surveyed and opened for settlement.

Many of the early settlers came from Ireland following the potato famines and from Scotland after the Highland Clearances. Travel was mainly along waterways, and settlers often landed at Cobourg where there was a sheltered harbour. The Irish settlers camped in tents along the shore in two areas that came to be called Corktown and Kerrytown.

The Empire Loyalists came north from New England following the American Revolution. They were offered free land providing they would take a loyalty oath. Clearing the land was back breaking work and the results can still be seen today where distinctive fieldstone walls still border the fields.

Settlers were unprepared for the frigid Canadian winters and many would have died without help from Ojibway Indians who were experienced in gathering wild rice, fishing and hunting, and often gave the newcomers food to survive. The Alderville First Nations Community was created in 1837. It is a thriving community and welcomes visitors to its cultural events. It is playing a lead role in recreating the Black Oak Savanna, the rare eco-system that existed before the European settlement. Well known members of the band include Fred Simpson, who represented Canada in the 1908 London Olympics

Cobourg Harbour after Hurricane Ernest. Photograph by Stephen Della Casa

Mist over the township. Photograph by Stephen Della Cassa

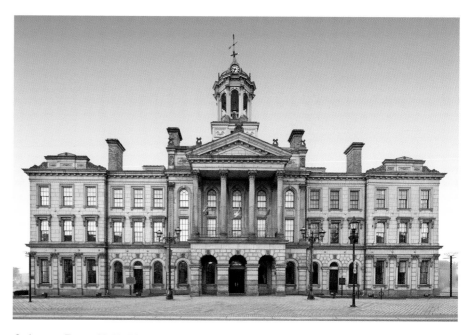

Cobourg Town Hall. Photograph by Jeff Gardner

placing sixth in the marathon, and Rick Beaver, an internationally recognized artist noted for his vibrant paintings of wildlife and native lifestyle.

In 1860 the Prince of Wales, later King Edward VII, opened the Cobourg to Peterborough railway which was intended to carry coal and iron ore to Cobourg on Lake Ontario. The Prince wisely declined to take the train across Rice Lake because of the precarious nature of the support structure and a few years later his suspicions were confirmed when the rail line was taken out by winter ice. The Prince also opened Cobourg's Victoria Hall - built in anticipation of a grand future as the Provincial capital - a dream that never materialized.

The early industries in Hamilton Township consisted of saw mills, dairy farming, road building and logging. Baltimore's most famous resident was a local preacher named Joseph Scriven who wrote the well- known hymn "What a Friend we have in Jesus".

The township is still a rural community. It has a fish culture station where lake and brook trout are raised. Dairy farming is still important. Latterly the character of the township has changed, however, because many of the older properties have been gentrified by retirees from Toronto, some of whom farm the land or rent out their properties to local farmers. This influx of retired professionals has led to a growth in cultural activities. Theatre and concerts are thriving. Tourism is important too. Outdoor activities such as fishing, hiking and biking abound, and the area has many attractive inns and health spas. The township is a haven for gardeners and nature lovers.

Text - Mike Hick

The Rolling Hills of Baltimore. Photograph by Stephen Della Cassa

Typical Ice Fishing Scene. Photograph by Mike Hick

HAMILTON RIVER (TOWN AND RIVER), NEWFOUNDLAND AND LABRADOR, 1821

Hamilton River (the town),since 1957 incorporated into Happy Valley-Goose Bay, is located at the mouth of the Churchill River (Hamilton River until 1965) in Central Labrador. Labrador is the northern portion of the Province of Newfoundland and Labrador on Canada's East Coast. The town and the adjacent river were named after Sir Charles Hamilton, the then Governor of Newfoundland in 1821 by Captain William Martin, RN.

The river, now called the Churchill River, flows for some 856 kilometres from Labrador's western extremes and is home to one of the world's largest underground Hydro Electric generating stations at Churchill Falls. Several more generating sites are being considered along its route. The region's indigenous population, the Innu, call the river "Mishtashipu" or "Grand River". Today the community is called Happy Valley-Goose Bay and is the largest populated centre in Labrador. There are several theories as

to how "Happy Valley" got its name, but one of the more interesting is that a visiting trapper from nearby Travespine arrived in town to spend time with a local female acquaintance. Apparently he had a most satisfactory visit and insisted that the town's name be changed to Happy Valley!

The area came to international prominence during the Second World War when the U.S. Government was granted a lease to establish an air base here as part of the "Lend Lease Program". The Air Base at nearby Goose Bay was originally constructed to facilitate Ferry Command to fly newly manufactured aircraft from North America to Europe for the war effort. The Air Base was in continuous use until the early 2000s serving the U.S. Air Force during the Cold War era and then home to several allied Air Forces who conducted low level tactical training over Labrador's vast and uninhabited areas.

Today, the town, the port and airport serve as a hub for all of Labrador facilitating tourism, transportation, and regional industrial development.

Text and Photographs by Geoff Goodyear

SIR CHARLES HAMILTON (1767 – 1849)

Sir Charles Hamilton, 2nd Baronet, was a British naval officer and governor of Newfoundland.

Hamilton was born in Britain in 1767. He began his naval career at the age of nine on his father's ship, the Hector, before attending the Royal Naval Academy at Portsmouth from 1777 to 1779. Hamilton commanded a number of vessels in the Royal Navy and was also a member of the British parliament on several occasions between 1790 and 1812 while still serving. He became baronet of Trebinshun on his father's death in 1784. From 1814 to 1817, he was Lieutenant Governor of Heligoland, a group of islands in the North Sea off the German coast.

He served as resident governor for the colony of Newfoundland from 1818 to 1823. During this period, he oversaw the reconstruction of St. John's following fires in 1818 and 1819. Although he was charged with promoting agriculture, he was soon discouraged by the poor soils of the island. The economy of the island was depressed due to decreased demand for Newfoundland cod and Hamilton encouraged diversification of the fisheries to include whales, seals and salmon.

Hamilton was made an Admiral on 22 July 1830, and died at the family home in Iping, West Sussex in 1849.

HAMILTON, ONTARIO, 1846

Hamilton, Ontario is a city of contrasts. Here lies a city most known for its history as Canada's Steel Town, an impression reinforced by the heavy industry facade that passers-by see as they drive over the Burlington Skyway Bridge that takes millions of vehicles from Toronto to Niagara Falls and the United States border, less than an hour away. This critical trade corridor is known as the "Golden Horseshoe" because almost 9 million people and a significant portion of the nation's businesses reside along the 200 kilometre route that follows the horseshoe shaped western end of Lake Ontario. From the Skyway, one is overwhelmed by the landscape of smokestacks and colossal rust coloured structures, despite the fact that the City of Hamilton is nestled into a stunning geographic setting and stretches many beautiful kilometres from the industrial core.

With the greenbelt and 90-metre cliff of the Niagara Escarpment creating a seam separating the upper and lower city, Hamilton offers naturally rugged green-space, spectacular waterfalls, wetlands and waterways. Once a visitor has had the privilege of discovering the "Real Hamilton", they will surely be impressed by its natural beauty and cultural offerings.

Like most of Canada, and the United States, the original inhabitants of the Hamilton area were the Native North American Aboriginal peoples. It is believed that European settlers first started visiting the region around the year 1620 and the townships at the "Head-of-The-Lake" were surveyed and named in the period from 1788-1793. Hamilton was incorporated as a city in 1846 and named after George Hamilton, who was a significant landowner in the area and was the first to draw plans for the new community shortly after the war of 1812.

Over the next 150 years Hamilton's population and business base grew at a rapid pace, as did the surrounding communities of Stoney Creek, Ancaster, Dundas, Famborough and Glanbrook, a group of five independent towns and villages, each with their own unique character and town centre. Inevitably, there came a time when the borders of the City of Hamilton and those of the adjoining communities became invisible for all practical purposes and a proposal was introduced to integrate the five towns and villages with the City of Hamilton. The idea was to create a mega city, made stronger by the efficiencies resulting from the streamlining of services. This concept was immediately met with considerable criticism and is still a contentious

issue for many, despite that amalgamation officially taking place in 2001. Each of the five amalgamated communities still take great pride in preserving their distinct identities, which makes the new City of Hamilton an even more appealing place to live, work and play.

With a population of more than 500,000, Hamilton is now the fourth largest city in the Province of Ontario (only Toronto, the Provincial Capital, Ottawa, the Nation's Capital and the city of Mississauga are larger) and the eighth largest in Canada, a country of over 30 million.

The amalgamated city is 1,117 square kilometres, of which a considerable amount is workable farmland, forest and protected green space. This is another example of the sharp contrast with its industrial reputation.

Many North American cities expanded rapidly and thrived during the industrial age and this only accelerated after the Second World War. Unfortunately, like so many of those cities, Hamilton's city core struggled terribly during the decline of the steel industry, the migration of manufacturing jobs to less expensive labour markets and finally, the mass exodus of residents and businesses to the newly developing phenomenon of the suburbs. Throughout the 1980s and 1990s the core of the city continued to erode. It must be noted, however, that even during the most difficult times, the downtown neighbourhood of "Durand" (where most of the fabulous wealth resided in the early part of last century, in equally fabulous mansions) maintained its ranking as one of the region's most prestigious places to live.

Over the past decade, several pockets around the city have received considerable investment from small business to create exciting street-centric identities. As these individual neighbourhoods become more prosperous, their spirit is spreading quickly to adjacent streets. Finally, Hamilton's downtown is turning around, organically, one block at a time.

Ottawa Street has long been one of the country's great textile districts, and now it also draws crowds to its farmers' market and is considered a top spot for antiquing.

Locke Street has taken on a traditional European feel and is a favourite with foodies, with its many restaurants, gourmet grocers, bakeries, boutiques and teahouses. It also hosts the Locke Street Festival, one of the city's many summer music and arts festivals.

Hess Village is a four block cluster of red brick Victorian homes most of which have been converted to nightclubs, pubs and restaurants. From May to October, Hess village is jam packed with sun worshippers occupying the endless patios during the day and a mix of live music and dance music fill the narrow pedestrian streets.

Westdale Village is a neighbourhood that supports the residential and commercial needs of the McMaster University students and faculty. The village has taken on the feel of a completely independent turn of the century British university town.

It is unlikely that you can spend more than a minute or two in a mall or busy street without seeing the black and yellow Hamilton Tiger Cats logo on a hat, jacket, t-shirt or bumper sticker. If there is one sport and one team that every Hamiltonian rallies around, it's their dearly loved "Ti-Cats", of the Canadian Football League.

Hamilton's broad ethnic and socioeconomic diversity has brought a wide variety of sports into the residents' lives. Soccer and baseball are played by all ages in every neighbourhood across town, as is ice hockey, one of Canada's most popular winter sports. Compounding the ice hockey fetish is the city's professional ice hockey team, the Hamilton Bulldogs of the American Hockey League.

Made possible by the proximity to Lake Ontario, watersports are very popular in the summer. The shoreline of Hamilton Harbour is dotted with no less than seven marinas and yacht clubs. The Leander Boat Club is a rowing club that has been consistently developing top athletes for over 125 years. Royal Hamilton Yacht Club has a rich history of yacht racing and has raised some of Canada's most successful sailors. RHYC's top-notch facilities, race committee and judges are known globally and they regularly host regional, national and world championship regattas in a variety of yacht classes.

One cannot write about sporting events in Hamilton without mentioning North America's longest running foot race, the "Around the Bay" race. The first Around the Bay race took place in 1894. The race takes participants through a gruelling course that takes advantage of the radical grade changes that the Niagara Escarpment demands of Hamilton roads. These same roads were used to run the 2003 UCI World Road Cycling Championships.

For a period of almost more than 50 years, Hamilton had an alpine ski centre within the city limits, thanks to the Niagara Escarpment. Despite the municipality shutting the Chedoke Winter Park down in 2003, those that learned here have created a significant community of skiing and snowboarding families who now make use of several alpine facilities within a short drive.

The property that hosted the winter park is the home to the Chedoke Civic Golf Club, a public course a few short blocks from City Hall. The crown jewel of the many

golf courses in the area is the Hamilton Golf and Country Club, established in 1894. As well as having been host to the PGA Canadian Open, this facility has a vibrant and stately past, including the weddings and parties for some of the most interesting characters in Hamilton's history.

The Niagara Escarpment is home to the Bruce trail, which is a pathway cut through some of the most populated areas of Ontario, including straight through the City of Hamilton. The trail starts at the Niagara River, not far from Niagara Falls, and meanders 885 kilometres to Tobermory, on Lake Huron. The trail has been named a UNESCO World Biosphere Reserve, so for those running, hiking, mountain biking or Nordic skiing on the path respect for this special environment is always a priority.

If it's a night on the town that you are looking for, countless live music venues, theatre productions and an international array of restaurants will serve your every taste. Pop, Rock and Blues acts fill the stages of the bar scene. The Hamilton Philharmonic and the Bach Elgar Choir offer a full range of classical and contemporary programmes, often featuring world-renowned guest performers. In recent years there has been an explosion of activity around the jazz genre, promoted in large part by the students and alumni of the Mohawk College jazz programme.

The vibe has spread and has attracted performers from around the globe to sit in with the local talent in both intimate club and theatre settings.

Hamilton has a vibrant visual arts community in the downtown core. Founded in 1914, the Art Gallery of Hamilton is one of Canada's largest public galleries and features over 9,500 works of art including European, historical Canadian and modern art. James Street North Village, which a decade ago was a struggling neighbourhood riddled with abandoned buildings, has been brought back to life in large part by the opening of several private art galleries and restaurants. The James Street North Art Crawl (taken from the "Pub Crawl" concept) is a regular event that has become very popular with art aficionados and the general public alike. On occasion, you may even be fortunate enough to catch a Jazz Crawl, a hybrid that brings live music to the galleries.

Hamilton has had some very distinctive waves of immigration over its history. Irish Immigrants first developed the Corktown neighborhood in the mid to late 1800s. During the first half of the last century, German, Polish and Ukrainian families came to Hamilton to make a new home for themselves. These cultures are still very much identifiable in the language, specialty merchants and celebrations that you will find around the city. In the 1960s a massive influx of Italian and Portuguese newcomers

arrived. Their strong cultural influence is most evident in the east end. Other than Canada's two official national languages (English and French), the language most often spoken in the city is Italian. More than 32,000 residents speak Italian, followed in popularity by Polish, Portuguese and Spanish.

The City of Hamilton is home to several outstanding post-secondary institutions that constantly receive accolades internationally for their research and exceptional contributions to their respective disciplines. The two most notable institutions are McMaster University, with over 25,000 students and 1,400 faculty, and Mohawk College, with 10,000 full time students, 3,000 apprentices and 42,000 continuing education students.

Over 150 million people live within a day's drive of Hamilton. Easy accessibility by rail, seaport, international airport (one of Canada's largest air cargo centres) and the 400 series highways make this city a natural North American logistics gateway.

Text – Jeff Schall

Photographs – Ron Scheffler – www.ronscheffler.com

GEORGE HAMILTON (1788 – 1836)

George Hamilton was a Canadian merchant and politician, who founded the city of Hamilton, Ontario.

Hamilton was born on October 1788 in Queenston Heights. He was the son of wealthy and influential Queenston merchant Robert Hamilton. Hamilton was educated in Edinburgh, Scotland and appears to have possessed a keen mind for business and letters. The Scottish schooling of the era would have exposed him to moral philosophy and what later became the separate discipline of economics. It is likely that his education fostered scepticism as well as a commitment to freedom of religion and the right to hold dissenting opinions, attitudes that would surface in his political career.

Hamilton also served during the War of 1812, where he held the rank of captain with the Niagara Light Dragoons, participating in the capture of Detroit and the Battle of Queenston Heights and Lundy's Lane. During 1814, British troops billeted at his Queenston establishment burned the property. This loss, combined with a familiarity with the Head of the Lake acquired during the war when Burlington Heights was heavily garrisoned, may have prompted George Hamilton's purchase of 257 acres of Barton Township in January 1815. Well placed and shrewd, Hamilton probably knew of pre-war discussions about creating a new administrative district with a judicial centre. Within a year of his land purchase, Hamilton reached agreement with the owner of adjacent property to the north, Nathaniel Hughson, on a scheme which they calculated would increase the possibility of having the court-house and jail for the new district located on Hamilton lands, to the benefit of the values of both men's property. Together they empowered James Durand to lobby at the House of Assembly for the Hamilton town site and to act as an agent selling town lots. The instructions coincided with the very week that the Assembly and Legislative Council deliberated on the formation of the new district and the designation of a district town. The act was passed on 22 March 1816. The precise manoeuvres cannot be documented, but there is little doubt that the origins of the Hamilton town site, and its location back from the waterfront, derived from a complicated private affair involving Hamilton, Hughson, and Durand. The new town was to become the capital of the new Gore District. Hamilton provided land for a courthouse and jail. The police village of Hamilton was incorporated in 1833. City status was achieved in 1846.

The offer they made to the government of Upper Canada included the granting of two blocks of land of two acres each to the Crown. These were to be reserved for the construction of public buildings. George Hamilton employed a grid street pattern used in most towns in Upper Canada and throughout the American frontier. The eighty original lots had frontages of fifty feet; each lot faced a broad street and backed onto a twelve-foot lane. It took at least a decade for all of the original lots to be sold, but the construction of the Burlington Canal in 1823, and a new court-house in 1827, encouraged Hamilton to add more blocks around 1828–29. At that time, he included a market square in an effort to draw commercial activity onto his lands, but the natural growth of the town was to the north of Hamilton's plot.

As a private town developer, Hamilton's record was mixed; he literally created the town, but he clearly tried to shape it to benefit his private fortunes. He did, however, leave enduring marks on the urban landscape; the court-house square, the haymarket, "the Gore", and the basic street plan of the city core.

Hamilton represented the riding of Wentworth in the Legislative Assembly of Upper Canada from 1821 to 1830, where he tended to support moderate reformers and encourage immigration to Canada. He helped set up a canal to link Hamilton harbour to Lake Ontario and worked to secure funding for the court house and jail.

Hamilton died on February 20, 1836. His body was buried at the family burial plot on the family's own farm. It is now part of Mountain Side Park.

Hamilton was one of a handful of important Canadians who recognized the colony's special needs and possibilities at an early date.

HAMILTON, PRINCE EDWARD ISLAND, 1869

Hamilton is a rural community situated on the perimeter of Malpeque Bay, Prince County, Prince Edward Island. The name Hamilton was adopted at a public meeting on 22 February 1869 to replace the names Oyster Cove and Shipyard, two adjacent communities which dated from the time of the early British settlers. The town was almost certainly named after Colonel John Hamilton Gray who was Premier of Prince Edward Island from 1863 – 1865. Hamilton has a long history, being in an area which was one of the earliest on the island to be settled under British regime. This settlement of Scottish immigrants began in 1770, the year that Walter Patterson, the first governor of Prince Edward Island, took up residence in the new colony. The area is a story of sturdy men and women who have built and shaped a community - their industry, valiant spirit and courage have helped to forge a province and a nation.

Hamilton became part of the Community of Malpeque Bay in 1973.

Photographs by Yolande Richard

Other Hamiltons in Canada

HAMILTON INLET

Hamilton Inlet is a fjord-like inlet on the Labrador coast of the Canadian province of Newfoundland and Labrador. Together with Lake Melville, it forms the province's largest estuary, extending over 140 kilometres inland to Happy Valley-Goose Bay and primarily draining the Churchill River (mentioned earlier in the Canada section) and Naskaupi River watersheds. Lake Melville is considered a part of Hamilton Inlet and extends west of the deep, narrow passage at the community of Rigolet. The inlet was named for Charles Hamilton, governor of Newfoundland 1818-24.

Mount Hamilton is an 8,503 feet mountain peak near Golden, British Columbia.

Mount Hamilton is a 5,872 feet mountain in Northern Territories.

Hamilton Hill is a 2,029 feet mountain peak near Provost, Alberta.

Hamilton Hill is a 1,589 feet mountain peak near Flin Flon, Manitoba.

Hamilton Mountain is an 815 feet mountain peak near Saint John, New Brunswick.

Hamilton Island, Nunavut, Canada is an unpopulated island in the Arctic north.

Hamilton Lake, Nova Scotia is situated in Halifax, Nova Scotia.

Hamilton Bank, off Newfoundland is a world famous fishing area for the North Atlantic Cod.

Hamilton Inlet. Photograph by Patrick Coutu

The Caribbean

HAMILTON PARISH, BERMUDA, 1608

Hamilton Parish (originally Bedford Parish) is one of the nine parishes of Bermuda. It was renamed for Scottish aristocrat James Hamilton, 2nd Marquis of Hamilton when he purchased the shares originally held in the Virginia Company by Lucy, Countess of Bedford. It is located in the northwest of the island chain, and is split in two by the large Harrington Sound, occupying all but the south and north eastern tip of its coast. The islands within the sound also form part of the parish. It is joined to Smith's Parish in the south and St. George's Parish in the northeast and covers just over 2.3 square miles.

Natural features in Hamilton include Flatts Inlet, Trunk Island, Shelly Bay, Bailey's Bay, Mangrove Lake, Trott's Pond, Crystal Cave, Castle Harbour, and The Causeway, which links Hamilton with St. George's Parish.

Notable locations in Hamilton include the Bermuda Aquarium and Museum and the small settlement of Flatts Village. Historically, the Colony's government had on occasion met in Flatts Village, rather than the then Capital of St. George's. The Village had prospered, in the days when the Colony's economy was seafaring, according to popular accounts, due to its distance from customs officials in St. George's.

Bailey's Bay, on the north shore of the Parish has also long been a thriving community, although it has never attained the status of a municipality. The name is used to denote an area which includes Callan Glen (named for shipbuilder Claud MacCallan), which is the shallow depression running north-eastward from Bailey's Bay, and that part of the Island running westward as far as Abbot's Cliff, on the Harrington Sound Shore. The area was long dominated by branches of the Outerbridge family (which includes the MacCallans). Notable landmarks include the Abbot's Cliff, Crystal Caves, and Mount Wyndham, once the location of Admiralty House, and from which the attack on Washington DC in 1815 was planned. Other sites of historical interest in the area include Tom Moore's Tavern (originally a private home, now a restaurant), and the adjacent nature reserve, and the western end of the Causeway. Other non-municipal 'communal areas' of Hamilton include the area around The Crawl, including Crawl Hill, and Shelly Bay.

The Coast of Callan Glen, Hamilton Parish

The Causeway. Photographs by James G Howes

JAMES HAMILTON, 2ND MARQUIS OF HAMILTON (1589 – 1625)

James Hamilton, 2nd Marquis of Hamilton and 4th Earl of Arran KG PC, styled Lord Aven from 1599 to 1604, was a Scottish politician. He was the son of John Hamilton, 1st Marquis of Hamilton.

He inherited his father's titles and estates in 1604. In 1608 he was created Lord Aberbrothwick, and the following year he inherited the earldom of Arran from his insane and childless uncle, James Hamilton. He moved to England with King James VI of Scotland, and invested into the Somers Isles Company, an offshoot of the Virginia Company, buying the shares of Lucy Harrington, Countess of Bedford. The Parish of Hamilton in Bermuda is named for him. He was created Earl of Cambridge and Baron of Innerdale in the peerage of England in 1619. In 1621 he served as Lord High Commissioner to the Parliament of Scotland, the King's representative in the Parliament of Scotland.

In 1603, he married Lady Ann Cunningham, a daughter of James Cunningham, 7th Earl of Glencairn and they had five children.

He also had an illegitimate daughter.

Hamilton died on 2 March 1625 at Whitehall, London, from a fever and was buried in the family mausoleum at Hamilton, Scotland, on 2 September of that year.

HAMILTON, BERMUDA, 1793

Hamilton, Bermuda, is one of the remotest capitals on Earth. These sub-tropical Atlantic islands, with an area of only some 23 square miles but with one of the world's densest populations of 64,000 people, are this planet's second most isolated, inhabited location (after St. Helena). Situated at the apex of the so-called "Bermuda Triangle", the nearest land-fall, Cape Hatteras in North Carolina, is 670 miles to the West, with Halifax, Nova Scotia, just over 700 miles North and the Bahamas and the West Indies a thousand miles or more to the South. Hamilton, Bermuda, is also one of the smallest capital cities, having an area of only 185 acres, or less than a square mile. (The Vatican is smallest.) While the city's resident population is less than 2,000, the day-time working population reaches about 13,500. That factor alone underscores how this little, remote place has also become a capital of international significance.

Founded in 1793, Hamilton became the capital in 1815, when the site of government moved from St. George's (capital since 1612) at these islands' eastern end, because of the impelling need for a centrally located port and administrative heart. The consecration of the Cathedral of the Most Holy Trinity (Church of England) in 1897 during Queen Victoria's Diamond Jubilee gave Hamilton the status of a city. The St. Theresa's Cathedral (Roman Catholic) is located just outside the northern city limits, but the main Wesleyan, African Methodist Episcopal, Seventh Day Adventist and Presbyterian churches and Salvation Army citadel are all to be found within city limits. Planning regulations ensure that the Bermuda Cathedral's imposing copper roof and tower continue to dominate the skyline.

The city is named after Captain Henry Hamilton, Governor from 1788 to 1794. He was instrumental in gathering the necessary support and driving through the legislation to create the town. In consequence, the city's coat of arms bears the motto "Hamilton sparsa collegit": "Hamilton brought together the scattered."

The City Hall was opened in February, 1960. This commanding, white structure is located on some of the city's high ground. While it is faithful to traditional Bermudian architecture, our only native art form, a Scandinavian influence can be seen in its tower (Stockholm's City Hall appears to have been a model). The tower is distinctive by not featuring a clock. Rather, it is graced by the "winds" of a compass whose needle responds to the movement of the weathervane. This weathervane takes the form of a model of the Sea Venture, Admiral Sir George Somers' ship, whose wrecking

Hamilton City Hall

Anglican Cathedral

on these islands (28th July, 1609), while sailing as flagship of a supply fleet bound for the English colony at Jamestown, began 400 years of British sovereignty. This ship also features in the city's crest and flag. In addition to housing the city's governmental and administrative functions, the building also includes a theatre, the Bermuda National Gallery and the gallery of the Bermuda Society of Arts. Hamilton's maritime connections are symbolized in a display of a collection of the crests of the many ships of the Royal Navy that have been posted here (for over 200 years Bermuda was headquarters of the Americas and West Indies Station), or have made Hamilton a port of call. There are military connections too. On the eastern boundary sits Fort Hamilton. This site, a reminder of Bermuda's nineteenth-century history as Britain's "Gibraltar of the West", is maintained as a visitor attraction offering stunning views over the city and the harbour.

Hamilton is the centre of Bermuda's governmental functions and political institutions. These islands maintain all the trappings of the Westminster parliamentary system, complete with political parties and cabinet government. The House of Assembly constitutes the legislative chamber for the 36 elected members of our lower house. Its two towers, with their Italianate decoration and with one sporting a four-faced clock (celebrating Victoria's Golden Jubilee), are prominent features of Hamilton's skyline. Nearby is the Georgian-styled Cabinet Building. Here meets the Government of the day as well as Bermuda's appointed upper house, the Senate. Also situated in this area are the Supreme and Magistrates Courts. On the grounds of the Cabinet Building may also be found a number of statues and monuments of local significance. Fronting the grounds is the Cenotaph (a smaller-scaled version of the original in Whitehall) commemorating Bermuda's 88 dead of the two World Wars. Another monument names the more than 2,000 who served then in the armed forces. The city also incorporates the Headquarters of Bermuda's Police and Fire Services, the National Library and Archives, the General Post Office as well as the bulk of the government ministries and departments. Owing to Bermuda's maintenance of a shipping registry, "Hamilton" is seen emblazoned on the stern-quarters of ships flying Bermuda's ensign, including vessels of the Cunard, P&O and Princess Cruise lines. Hamilton also serves as the home of Bermuda's registry of aircraft.

As the major port, Hamilton's docks sit right along-side Front Street, which, as the name suggests, is Hamilton's main business street. The buildings lend Hamilton its distinctive harbour-side character. Its focal point is the flagpole, before which take place ceremonial parades, including "Beat Retreats" performed by the Band of the Bermuda Regiment and the Bermuda Islands Pipe Band. Here tie up those cruise

House of Assembly

Front Street with Police Stand

ships able to negotiate Hamilton Harbour's restricted entrance and manoeuvring space. (Today's much larger "Panamax" cruise ships utilize the re-developed docking facilities of the former Royal Navy Dockyard at the islands' west end.) From here also the ferry services ply the waters of the harbour and head for the east and west ends of the islands. Hamilton is the main shopping centre for visitors and residents alike, but branches of the great retail chains encountered overseas will not be found: Bermuda law requires 60% Bermudian ownership. There are no major hotels within the city. (The Hamilton Hotel, the first "proper" hostelry, opened in 1851; after several major regenerations – welfare centre for soldiers and sailors in World War II, then Government offices – the building burned down in December, 1955.) Immediately to the west, however, is the famous Princess Hotel, whose opening in 1884 is taken to be the beginning of Bermuda's renowned history as a major tourist destination. (The Bermudiana, another major hotel on the western limits, was destroyed by fire, rebuilt, and finally demolished to become the site of two of Bermuda's largest international insurance companies.) As would be expected of a capital city, Hamilton is home to the major international service clubs: Rotary; Lions; and Kiwanis. The oldest, Hamilton Rotary Club, was founded in 1924.

The city's streets received their names in 1849. While some are functional and descriptive (Front; Church; Court; Parliament; Park; North), others have been named after former governors (Reid; Dundonald; Elliot; Laffan) or have royal associations (Victoria; Queen; King; Princess; Brunswick). The city boasts two spacious (for Hamilton!) parks, Par-la-Ville and Victoria; the latter contains the restored bandstand erected in 1887 to commemorate Queen Victoria's Golden Jubilee. Another smaller, harbour-side park, Albuoy's Point, is a favourite spot for viewing the port's comings and goings as well as sailing contests, including those of Bermuda's unique dinghies, referred to as "acrobatic sailing". On the park's western side sits the Royal Bermuda Yacht Club, founded in 1844 by a coalition of naval and military officers with Hamilton's merchant elite. The Royal Hamilton Amateur Dinghy Club, however, is located across the harbour in Paget Parish. Albuoy's Point is also the site of a memorial to HMS Jervis Bay, an Armed Merchant Cruiser serving on the Bermuda-Halifax Convoy Force in the early years of the Second World War. She was destroyed (5th November, 1940) in a heroically sacrificial engagement with the German "pocket battleship" Admiral Scheer, successfully saving her convoy.

Hamilton, Bermuda, has become one of the world's three largest insurance markets. With some 400 of 1,600 domiciled international companies having a physical presence, international business constitutes more than 80% of Bermuda's economy. Indeed,

Bermuda Harbour

Hamilton's financial clout is dominated by the insurance sector. According to the Bermuda Monetary Authority, at the end of the latest (2010) statutory reporting period, 950 companies had total assets of $524 billion and had written gross premiums of over $107 billion. (Investment funds and banking account for another $100 billion.) Twelve of the world's top 40 insurance and re-insurance multi-nationals – from ACE Limited to XL Capital Ltd – operate from Hamilton. This little city commands 36% of the global insurance market. Since the arrival in 1947 of American International Company, Hamilton, Bermuda, has evolved from primarily a domicile for captives in the period before the 1980s to being by the early 1990s a reinsurance market for excess liability and property catastrophe insurance (ACE; XL) and to its present status as the "risk capital of the world" taking on all types of insurable risks.

Hamilton's reputation as a world centre of business rests on a fundamental principle: Bermuda-based companies face few restrictions on how they may invest their assets and deploy their capital. Most important to the companies' presence here, however, is the fact that they operate in a Commonwealth, common law constituency and have the right of ultimate appeal to the Judicial Committee of the Privy Council in London.

Bermuda Harbour

In case of legal dispute, therefore, they have recourse to a juridical process unaffected by local political influences. Further, relative ease of incorporation is combined with a collaborative, commercially sensible regulatory regime. A sophisticated infrastructure has been built up over the years: Hamilton's professional organizations offer communications, banking, legal, actuarial and auditing (there are some 500 certified accountants) services of the required international standard. Hamilton also turns out to be ideally geographically located to conduct business in major markets, being four hours behind London and one hour ahead of New York. Whilst operating in a global market, even the CEO's of these great international companies can be seen on the streets of Hamilton sporting our iconic business attire of sometimes vivid (pink; yellow; lime green) Bermuda shorts, knee-length hose (both of which – but not the colour – originate with the British forces) and blue blazers. Many of their employees soon also learn to appreciate the local libation of black rum and ginger beer (known in Hamilton's watering-holes as "dark and stormy" but originating in the Royal Navy's rum tot irreverently dubbed by the matelots as "Nelson's blood"), as well as being able to savour the international cuisine offered in Hamilton's restaurants.

Significantly also, Bermuda remains a dependent territory of the United Kingdom: Hamilton is the capital of the most populous of the remnants of the former British Empire. As a responsible, self-governing jurisdiction, Bermuda functions under her own constitution which provides the attributes of a modern state and which bestows authority in all local affairs, including immigration and safety. These powers provide the foundations for the continuance of political stability and the maintenance of the environment within which the international companies can confidently operate. The Governor, as the Queen's representative, provides the main channel for communication, and liaison, with London and retains responsibility for most aspects of internal security, external defence and foreign affairs. Bermuda's Government, by concluding taxation agreements and information-sharing protocols with other countries and overseas bodies, is able to combat illegal activity and the "tax haven" appellation sometimes employed by those unfamiliar with the legal and political regime based in Hamilton.

Hamilton, Bermuda, may be minute amongst capital cities; but Hamilton, Bermuda, is also a capital with an international presence.

Above Left: Cabinet Building and War Memorial
Above Right: Harbour View
Photographs by David Rowntree
Text – Dr George L. Cook

HENRY HAMILTON (1734 – 1796)

Henry Hamilton was an Irish-born soldier and official of the British Empire. He was captured during the American War of Independence while serving as the Lieutenant Governor at the British post of Fort Detroit.

Henry was probably born in Dublin, Ireland, a younger son of Henry Hamilton, an Irish Member of Parliament. He was raised in County Cork and started his military career during the French and Indian War, as a Captain in the 15th Regiment of Foot in the 1757 attack on Louisbourg and the Battle of Quebec. With the support of the Lieutenant Governor of Canada, Guy Carleton, Hamilton rose to the rank of Brigade Major. In 1775, he sold his commission, leaving the British Army for a political career.

In 1775, Hamilton was appointed Lieutenant Governor and Superintendent of Indian Affairs at Fort Detroit, one of five newly created lieutenant governorships in the recently expanded Province of Quebec. The American Revolutionary War was already underway by the time Hamilton arrived at Detroit to assume his duties. Hamilton was in a difficult position: as a civil official, Hamilton had few regular troops at his command, and the natives of the region—French Canadians and American Indians— were not all supporters of the British regime.

Hamilton became adept at diplomacy with American Indians, establishing good relations with local Indian leaders. Hamilton, an amateur artist, sketched portraits of many Native Americans while in Detroit, leaving what has been called the "earliest and largest collection of life portraits of Native Americans of the Upper Great Lakes." When the war began, British officials initially determined not to enlist Indians as allies in the war effort, but in 1777 Hamilton received instructions to encourage Indian raids against the American frontier settlements of Virginia and Pennsylvania. This was a controversial policy because it was realised that civilian colonists would inevitably be killed in these raids. Hamilton attempted to limit civilian casualties by sending British officers and French-Canadian militia with the American Indian war parties. Nevertheless, hundreds of settlers in Kentucky and western Pennsylvania were killed and scalped by raiding parties during the war. In Detroit, Hamilton is alleged to have paid bounties for prisoners and scalps brought in by the Indians (no positive proof was ever found to support this claim, however). He became hated by American settlers, who dubbed him the "Hair-buyer General of Detroit".

Above Right: Hamilton surrenders to Clark at Vincennes

In 1778, Virginia forces under Colonel George Rogers Clark captured several undermanned British posts in the Illinois country, including Fort Sackville at Vincennes. Hamilton set out from Detroit on 7 October 1778 to recapture the post, 600 miles away. His small force gathered Native American allies along the way, and entered Vincennes on 17 December 1778, capturing Fort Sackville and the American commandant, Captain Leonard Helm. In February 1779, however, Colonel Clark returned to Vincennes in a surprise march, recapturing the outpost and taking Hamilton prisoner.

Because of his support of the Indian raids, the Virginians regarded Hamilton as a war criminal rather than a conventional prisoner of war. Clark sent Hamilton to Williamsburg, Virginia, where he was jailed and often kept in irons by Governor Thomas Jefferson. Jefferson finally granted Hamilton parole at the instructions of General George Washington. In early 1781, Hamilton was exchanged and travelled to London.

Hamilton returned to Canada in 1782, becoming Lieutenant-Governor, and later Deputy-Governor of Quebec. He went on to serve as Governor of Bermuda from 1788 to 1794, and of Dominica from 1794 until his death on the island of Antigua in 1796.

View from Hamilton Fort. Photograph supplied by St Vincent and the Grenadines Tourism Board

On the northern point of Admiralty Bay, beyond Hamilton Village, is Hamilton Fort. The site of Hamilton Fort in Bequia, built in the late 18th Century by the French to protect the harbour approach from the English, provides a fantastic view over Admiralty Bay towards Port Elizabeth and Princess Margaret Beach. The original structure is long gone, but both French and English cannon salvaged from the waters around Bequia, are now placed there and the walk from Port Elizabeth is made worthwhile by the amazing views. The defence of the entrance to Admiralty Bay was also a priority for the British. In 1771, the harbour was described as being "very fine, where Ships of Force may safely ride", and ideal for careening (no such harbour existed in St. Vincent).

Due south of Hamilton Fort, on the small headland above Lower Bay, there was a second fortification, and the approach from St. Vincent was covered by additional emplacements a few hundred feet north of Hamilton Fort. Eleven cannon in all were recommended for these three batteries, at a total estimated cost of 1,500 pounds - a huge sum in those days.

HAMILTON FORT, BEQUIA, ST VINCENT AND THE GRENADINES

James Hamilton, father of Alexander Hamilton, moved from St. Croix, where he had raised Alexander as his son, to Bequia in 1774 under a programme instituted by Great Britain to give land to indigent settlers. The land granted to Hamilton lies along the shore of Southeast Bay. The elder Hamilton lived in Bequia until 1790 but was never visited by his son nor did he visit Alexander in America, despite the latter's frequent gifts of money and entreaties to immigrate or at least visit him.

Today along the north shore of Admiralty Bay, just outside of Port Elizabeth and on the way to Hamilton Fort, is the small fishing village of Hamilton. It nestles into the hillside with its colourful houses and tiny Roman Catholic Church. A number of boats pull up on the sandy shore and small rum shops dot the roadside.

Other Hamiltons In the Caribbean

HAMILTONS VILLAGE, ANTIGUA AND BARBUDA

Hamiltons Village is a place with a very small population in the region of Saint John, Antigua and Barbuda.

HAMILTON, ST KITTS AND NEVIS

A number of places on St Kitts bear the name of Hamilton after Alexander Hamilton who was born on St Kitts.

Site of Alexander Hamilton's birth – now Museum of Nevis History.
Photograph by Daniel Farrell

Australia

HAMILTON, TASMANIA, 1824

Hamilton is a pretty town on the Clyde River with views of mountain ranges to the west. The town and surrounding area has a population of around 300.

Located 74 kilometres northwest of Hobart on the Lyell Highway, Hamilton is a typical Tasmanian Historic Town combining a setting which dates to the early nineteenth century with a range of historic accommodation. It is relatively unspoilt and still sufficiently removed from over-commercialisation to offer the visitor an opportunity to experience what the villages of southern Tasmania were like in the 1830s and 1840s.

The area was settled by Scottish farmers and you can still find the cottages and grand old farm houses once inhabited by the early farmers. Hamilton developed as a transport hub and by the 1830s was operating a number of breweries and a roaring illegal spirits trade. The early settlers had big visions and the street foundations reveal the town they dreamt of establishing. It was once destined to be the capital of Tasmania despite its vast distance from any port.

The first Europeans into the Hamilton area were the botanist, Robert Brown and his party who attempted to trace the Derwent River to its source in March, 1804. They reached the Hamilton Plains and followed the Fat Doe River (now known as the Clyde) up to the Clyde Falls near the present site of Bothwell.

Hamilton's proximity to Hobart Town meant that the region was visited regularly by search parties, escaped convicts and bushrangers. By the late 1830s the land had been divided and settled.

Governor Macquarie named the locality as 'Sorell Plains', and it became locally known as 'Macquarie' and 'Lower Clyde'. Governor Arthur finalised a name for the locality in 1824.

Hamilton Panorama. Photograph by Appleisle

St Peter's Church. Photograph by Tristan Kleinschmidt

Cumberland Street. Photograph supplied by Central Highlands Council

A typical Hamilton Cottage. Photograph by Appleisle

Glen Clyde House. Photograph by Appleisle

There are a number of conflicting explanations for the town's name. Some sources claim that it was named Hamilton by Governor Macquarie in 1821 while others claim that in 1829 Governor Arthur named the district after his friend William Henry Hamilton, the Hobart Town Postal Officer. Whatever the origins the town was known as Hamilton by 1835 and by 1859 a traveller could describe the town as 'Here is a neat Church, a handsome bridge, large inns, breweries and some good shops. And round the village are some of the largest landed proprietors in the country possessing 20,000 and even as many as 40,000 sheep'. Hamilton was declared a municipality in 1863.

This sleepy little village has a number of historic buildings. The most important are St Peter's Church (consecrated in 1838), Glen Clyde House (1840), now a craft gallery, and the accommodation at the Old Schoolhouse (1856), Emma's Cottage (1830), George's Cottage (1845), Victoria's Cottage (1845) and the Hamilton Inn (1834).

The foundation stone for St Peter's Church was laid in 1834. It was completed in 1837 and consecrated by Bishop Broughton, the only Bishop of Australia, on 8 May 1838.

It is worth noting that the church has only one door. The reason for this was almost certainly to prevent the congregation, which in the early days was about 50 per cent convicts, from attempting to escape. The original church was a simple stone building. There were plans to add a spire to the tower in the 1920s but they never eventuated.

Hamilton Heritage Centre. Photograph by Tristan Kleinschmidt

The Old Schoolhouse, a two storey structure, was built by convict stonemasons in 1858. It is an interesting comment on the times that it was originally constructed so that the Headmaster lived in the room above the central staircase and the children, according to their sex, entered the school from different doors. It was seriously deteriorating and was condemned to be demolished in the early 1970s but its restoration has made it one of Hamilton's most unusual and charming places to stay.

The three cottages, Emma's, Victoria's and George's, also offer interesting historic accommodation. Like the Old Schoolhouse they were all built of local sandstone by convicts. Their current owner's passion for antiques has meant that they are probably better furnished now than they were when the first residents moved in.

Jackson's Emporium was built in 1856. This sandstone shop was the Centre of Commerce in colonial Hamilton and has now re-opened as an interesting and different kind of department store specialising in Derwent Valley products.

The appeal of Hamilton, which is a truly charming village, is based on its peacefulness and its outstanding range of historic accommodation. It also has an excellent fishing and aquatic area at Lake Meadowbank.

The Old School House with newer version. Photograph by Tristan Kleinschmidt

Prospect Villa. Photograph by Appleisle

Clyde River in flood. Photograph supplied by Central Highlands Council

HAMILTON HILL, PERTH, W.AUSTRALIA, 1830

Hamilton Hill is a suburb of Perth, Western Australia, 14 miles Southwest of the CBD.

The earliest known settler at Hamilton Hill was Sydney Smith, the agent of Captain George Robb, who arrived in Western Australia in 1830 and took up land south of Fremantle. Smith and Robb had come to Australia on the Leda, a ship owned by the Hamilton Ross Company of Cape Town. During the next twelve months Smith was actively engaged in establishing Robb's farm. In a letter dated 27 August 1830, he gives his address as Hamilton Hill. Whether it was Robb or Smith who did the naming after the firm, remains uncertain but the area has been known as such ever since.

In 1860 Charles Alexander Manning bought 364 hectares of Robb's land, and six years later built Davilak House for his son Lucius Manning. The twelve roomed house was built using convict labour and was owned by the Manning family until they abandoned it in the late 1950s. It burnt down in 1960, and after this the Shire of Cockburn took over the administration of the whole estate.

Manning Lake in Hamilton Hill.
Photograph provided by mark_ncompass on panoramio.com

Manning Park and Azelia Ley Homestead Museum.
Photograph by Mike Tortolano

Hamilton Hill Memorial Hall. Photograph by Gnangarra

A second homestead was built in 1920 by Azelia Ley, the eldest daughter of Lucius Manning. She had married John Morgan Ley in 1900, and after he died in 1927 she continued to maintain the family farm. This house became derelict after Azelia died in 1954, but was restored by the Historical Society of Cockburn in 1983 and now serves as a comprehensive Azelia Ley Homestead Museum of artefacts pertaining to the Cockburn district.

HAMILTON ROSS (1774 – 1853)

Hamilton Ross was one of the most prominent early businessmen of Irish birth.

He was born in Galway in 1774. He joined the Aberdeenshire Rifles as an ensign at the age of 15 and participated in the capture of the Cape in 1795. Having eloped with a Dutch heiress, he became a merchant and amassed a great fortune. He moved to South Africa and founded the leading firm of merchants Hamilton Ross and Company in Cape Town in 1806. By 1818 he had twelve slaves, three carriages and five horses. Soon he was to own Cape Town's first merchant fleet as the company handled exports of grain and wine from the Cape, imports from India and other places and was responsible for keeping Mauritius, Reunion and St Helena provisioned. Ross was one of the founders of the Cape of Good Hope Bank in 1826 and continued to play an active role in Cape Town's business life until the late 1840s.

He was one of the few British settlers who were fully bilingual and he moved the first resolution which resulted in Natal being incorporated into the British Empire. His house was eventually sold by his nephew John Ross to the Castle Steamship company in 1894 and was rebuilt to become Cape Town's foremost hotel.

HAMILTON, VICTORIA, 1854

Hamilton was built near the border of three traditional tribal territories: the Gunditjmara land that stretches south to the coast, the Tjapwurong land to the north east and the Bunganditj territory to the west. People who lived in these areas tended to be settled rather than nomadic. The region was, and is, fertile and well-watered, leading to an abundance of wildlife, and no need to travel far for food. Physical remains such as the weirs and fish traps found in Lake Condah to the south of Hamilton, as well as the accounts of early white settlers, support local indigenous oral histories of well-established settlements in the area.

On 12 September 1836, the explorer, Major Thomas Mitchell was the first European to travel through the area where Hamilton later developed. His reports of the fertility and abundance of 'Australia Felix' (as he called this region of Western Victoria) encouraged pastoralists to move to the area and establish large sheep runs. By 1839 there were a number of settlers in the area including the Wedge family, whose property 'The Grange' was located within the present town site.

The proximity of The Grange to other properties and to important tracks between Portland and New South Wales led to the gradual emergence of a small town. This included an inn, blacksmith, a small store and some shanties and businesses nearby. The site was a small social centre for surrounding pastoral properties, with horse races being held along the Grange Burn flat.

The desire for a school prompted a town survey that commenced in 1849. The township of Hamilton was formally declared in 1851. The town was named in the following way as quoted by the book, "Dundas Shire Centenary 1863-1963". "In 1840, owing to police difficulties in controlling public houses on, or not on the imaginary boundary line, Henry Wade was sent from Sydney on a special mission to mark out the boundary. He completed the survey as far as Serviceton by the spring of 1847, and was then appointed District Surveyor and in 1850, laid out a township for the Grange, which he named Hamilton. It was then the prerogative of the surveyor to christen his lay-out. Wade and his family had made close friends of the Hamiltons of Bringalbert, there being intermarriages later." The Hamilton family ran Bringalbert Station, largely rearing horses. A number of aborigines, taught by Thomas Hamilton of Bringalbert, were included in the Aborigine Cricket tour to England in 1868, the first team from Australia to tour England.

Gray Street, Hamilton. Photograph by Dave Napper

The railway reached the town in 1877.

Hamilton today has a population of 10,450. Hamilton enjoys a moderate climate with average temperatures of 26 degrees in summer and 12 degrees in winter.

The Grampians National Park is the main draw card for the region. Declared a National Park in 1984, it is an oasis of diversity, set amongst the agricultural Western District of Victoria. The 167,000 acres house around a third of Victoria's plant species, and form a safe haven for many species of marsupial and mammal.

The region has become immensely popular with a wide demographic, and understandably so - the park has something to offer everyone. Outlandish rock architecture is covered with gently undulating native forest . . . wildlife is abundant and viewable . . . the air is crisp . . . and during spring, the park vibrates with colour.

Hamilton is part of a large volcanic region called Kanawinka which includes two fantastic waterfalls called Wannon and Nigretta. As the centre of a massive and wealthy pastoral industry for over 160 years, Hamilton has become a thriving country city. Although filled with cultural experiences, Hamilton provides a first- hand opportunity for the traveller to experience the everyday life of a bustling country centre. Excellent shopping, diverse architecture, a fascinating art gallery and stunning botanic gardens are just the beginning of your Hamilton experience. Its position makes the perfect launching pad for any stay in the Southern Grampians, but you would be wise to spend time in this city as the joys of Hamilton takes some time to explore.

Whether it's gazing at botanical, artistic or architectural beauty, putting in a bid as part of a 50,000-head sheep sale or just browsing through great shops, Hamilton offers an amazing array of experiences for all travellers. Hamilton embodies a strong community spirit; an innovative, creative and entrepreneurial population; a wealth of natural assets and education and health facilities that are the envy of other cities of a similar population.

Hamilton College

Hamilton Streetscape at night

Various shots of Kangaroos and Dingo around Hamilton

Nigretta Falls in Grampian National Park

While other major centres in Victoria were being built on gold, Hamilton was built on wool and the finest of its type in the world. A fifty kilometre radius around the city yields more sheep per hectare than anywhere else on the planet, previously earning Hamilton the title "the wool capital of the world." A drive around the region will confirm this but will also introduce you to the many other industries that make Hamilton a country city that continues to thrive both economically and culturally. From a very early age the town earned a reputation as "the collegiate city" given the very high standard of education offered by the various secondary schools.

Hamilton oozes with style and quality, a few quiet minutes walking amongst the enormous English Oaks and pines, fountains and rotunda in the botanical gardens will calm and enchant you. Many of the original trees are classified by the National Trust. You will have no trouble finding the very large English Oak that was planted in 1892, the largest known example of the species in the state. Interestingly, it is not the oldest tree in the vast gardens with some of the exotic pine trees planted before this time.

The curator of the Melbourne Botanical Gardens, William Guilfoyle, drew up new plans for the gardens in 1881, about ten years after the first plantings took place. He included the current lake, which is no longer home to the white swans that were introduced at about this time. The gardens are a reminder of how homesick the early European settlers were, as although the district is home to native grasslands and towering forests, the gardens remind you of English grandeur. The gardens are the perfect spot to spend a fun afternoon with children as acres of well -manicured lawns invite games and picnics. The innovative walk-through aviary is home to many exotic and native birds while kangaroos, emus and wallabies also reside in the gardens. Those that designed, built and nurtured the Hamilton Botanic Gardens over the last 150 years would be very proud of how this stunning sanctuary is presented today.

Above Right: Hamilton Post Office
Below Right: Gray Spires, Hamilton, Victoria

191

Lake Hamilton

Wannon Falls

Treasures await you at another of Hamilton's main attractions. The rich and diverse collection of paintings and decorative arts at the Hamilton Art Gallery is well worth a visit. Highlights include the fabulous Shaw Bequest left to the city in 1957 and now considered to be one of Australia's major arts bequests of the 20th century. You will also discover on permanent display an important collection of 29 paintings by 18th century English artist, Paul Sandby, known as the 'Father of English Watercolour'. Six galleries feature ever changing exhibitions of historic and contemporary works. You can enjoy outstanding English and European silver, porcelain and glass, Asian ceramics and bronzes, paintings and prints as well as a small collection of furniture.

Dingo Photograph – Les Diamond
Text and Other Photographs – Hamilton Tourism

The buildings which remain in Main Street, Hamilton, South Australia
Photograph by Elaine Kidner

HAMILTON, SOUTH AUSTRALIA, 1855

Hamilton is a small township in the Mount Lofty Ranges in South Australia. It is about 120 kilometres northeast of Adelaide, about 20 kilometres north of Kapunda.

Hamilton owes its origin to the discovery of copper at Burra in 1845. The town was built to cater for the passing wagon teams travelling from Burra to Port Adelaide and later, when the railway reached the area, to Kapunda.

In 1849 George Robertson bought 89 acres, at one pound per acre, in "The Valley of the River Light." The town was officially registered as Hamilton in 1855, Robertson naming the town after his birthplace of Hamilton in Scotland.

By 1866 there was a population of 200 with two stores, a schoolroom, two churches and a post office. A reasonable sized community existed throughout the first half of the 20th century, despite electricity not reaching the town until 1960.

Today, however, there is little evidence of much of Hamilton's past. St Matthew's Church is really the sole survivor of its grander times.

HAMILTON DOWNS STATION, NORTHERN, TERRITORIES, 1860

Hamilton Downs Station takes its name from a spring, in the headwaters of the Jay Creek, discovered by Australian explorer John McDouall Stuart in 1860.

Stuart has been described as Australia's greatest inland explorer. He and his companions in 1862 completed the first European crossing of Australia from Adelaide to Van Diemen Gulf, passing through the centre and returning safely along the same route. Using horses, and travelling lightly and quickly, Stuart established a 'new' method of exploration, and named many of the landmarks of Central Australia.

Jay Creek is a normally dry water course that with rain in the catchment area becomes a torrent wall of water flowing out into the red desert.

Hamilton Downs recognises George Hamilton, a prominent South Australian who supported Stuart's three expeditions between 1860 and 1862.

The Station was established just before World War 1 by Sid Stanes Jnr. and Ted Harris. Stanes had worked at various jobs in the early 1900s including cook at the Alice Springs Telegraph Station (1904-1905) and manager of the Stuart Arms Hotel (1907).

In 1909 he entered into some agreement with Ted Harris, formerly of Broken Hill, to take on some pastoral country in the hills north and west of Alice Springs. By 1913 they had settled on the homestead site and given it the name Hamilton Downs Station.

In the early years Stanes and Harris made their money by mustering Brumbies (wild horses) running wild in the hills and gullies of the MacDonnell Ranges. At this time horses were worth more than cattle because of the war-time need for cavalry and horse drawn artillery. However, it lasted long enough to give them a good start.

In 1920 Stanes sold his share of the station to Harris and bought Erldunda Station. In 1923 Harris married Emily Francis from the Oodnadatta area and she joined him on the property in 1924. Two years later, however, they sold the station to Sydney Kidman and moved south to Adelaide.

The Old House at Hamilton Downs

Solar Power at Hamilton Downs

The station was subsequently managed by Charlie Wright (for Kidman) from 1927 until 1929 when Harris bought it back again in partnership with the Davis family. (Harris held a half share and three Davis brothers held one sixth each). Harris maintained his share in the station until the 1940s when he sold out to the Davis brothers.

In 1948 the old Homestead was abandoned and a new one established in a more accessible site to the northwest. Damien Miller bought an interest in the property in 1952 and acquired sole ownership in 1968.

The old homestead buildings lay in ruins from 1948 until 1972 when the Apex Club of Central Australia took on the task of restoring them and converting the site to a youth camp. The Hamilton Downs Youth Camp was officially opened on 11th March 1978.

Around Hamilton Downs Station

A waterhole at Chewing Range, Hamilton Downs

In October 1980 the Hamilton Downs Youth Camp was entered in the Register of the National Estate, this is defined in the Australian Heritage Commission Act 1975 as: those places that have aesthetic, historic, scientific or social significance or other special value for the next generation and present.

The Hamilton Downs Youth Camp continues to grow as a Youth camp providing a rural retreat for school and other groups to learn of the history of the pastoral development in Central Australia, Aboriginal culture and the environment. http://www.hamiltondownsyouthcamp.org.au/index.htm

It is interesting to note that of recent times (2011) Hamilton Downs station is now back with the Davis family with the purchase in 2011 by Anthony and Pam Davis.

Text and Photographs – Renton Kelly

Rains that broke the drought

GEORGE HAMILTON (1812 – 1883)

George Hamilton, police commissioner, was born on 12 March 1812, probably in Hertfordshire, England, one of at least eight children of Charles Hamilton. Following education at Harrow School in 1823-26, George served in the navy as a midshipman. He reached Sydney before 1837, at which time he overlanded sheep to Australia Felix. In 1839, following Charles Bonney's southern route, he drove cattle to Adelaide.

He began mixed farming in partnership with Arthur Hardy while venturing, with scant success, into commerce and lithography, and visiting Melbourne in 1846. The next year he helped to organize the first exhibition of South Australian artists' works, including some of his own. A founding member of the South Australian Society of Arts in 1856 he won and gave prizes, and later acted as a judge, at its exhibitions. He contributed some of the illustrations for published journals of exploration by Sir George Grey and E. J. Eyre.

Hamilton became a clerk in the South Australian Treasury in 1848 and Inspector of Mounted Police in 1853. His duty took him on a journey in 1859 to the far north with the governor Sir Richard MacDonnell, whom he considered a blustering humbug. Hamilton had to do the work of the police commissioner P. E. Warburton, as well as his own, while the latter was away on exploring expeditions, and organized the fitting out of the last two expeditions of John McDouall Stuart. In 1867 Warburton was removed from office and Hamilton became commissioner, surviving public criticism and two parliamentary inquiries. His prudent management during financial stringency led to expansion later, including the re-establishment of a detective unit and the use of camels in the far north.

As an active member of the Acclimatization Society (later Royal Zoological Society of South Australia), he was invited in 1881 to advise a parliamentary committee on sparrows, which were causing financial loss to farmers. He favoured a bounty on sparrows and their eggs to reduce their numbers.

From 1848 Hamilton had contributed stories, verse and topical essays to Adelaide periodicals. His reminiscences, originally serialized, were published in 1879 as Experiences of a Colonist Forty Years Ago, and A Journey from Port Phillip to South Australia in 1839, by 'An Old Hand', and reprinted the following year with A Voyage from Port Phillip to Adelaide in 1846. Hamilton's most ambitious poem, of about fifty pages, published in 1868, was Pscycos and Phrenia, or the World before Man's Advent, giving a romantic account of evolution to the point where 'Man' suddenly makes his appearance. In 1864-77 he published three booklets on horses, denouncing the cruel methods commonly used for breaking them in and advocating improved methods of shoeing and stabling. His books were illustrated with lithographs and photographic prints from his own drawings.

Hamilton's writings contain vivid descriptive passages and whimsical comments on human foibles. His pictures capture the horse in all its moods and, like his narratives, include valuable historical information. He is not among the first ranks of Australian painters, poets or authors, but is better than most of his amateur contemporaries in all these fields.

Energetic, ambitious and a strict but fair disciplinarian, Hamilton was nonetheless noted for his genial nature, and some of his poetry was quite sentimental. His expert knowledge of horses enabled him to raise the standard of the Mounted Police so that it became an attractive occupation for 'well-bred young men'. He helped to organize hunt meets and was a principal founder of the Adelaide Club, which became his home. He did not marry. Hamilton retired in 1882 and died on 2 August 1883 at Burnside.

Looking East down Hamilton Reach. Photograph by Carol Springer

HAMILTON, BRISBANE, 1865

Hamilton is said to be named after the proprietor of the Hamilton Hotel, Mr Gustavus Hamilton. It is situated on the banks of the Brisbane River approximately 7 kilometres north of Brisbane CBD.

In the early days of the Moreton Bay settlement Hamilton continued to be a popular camping site for aboriginal tribes, one of them being the Bribie tribe. The last big battle between the warlike Bribie tribe and the local Bunya Bunya tribe took place about the junction of what is now Toorak Road with Kingsford Smith Drive. After that the Bunya Bunya tribe seems to have broken up.

When the penal settlement was started in Brisbane the female convicts were housed on the site which is now the Brisbane General Post Office, then in 1837 they were

Brisbane Ferry at Hamilton North Shore. Photograph by Australand

moved to the Eagle Farm area where they grew maize and vegetables, and were largely responsible for keeping the settlement in food.

A road was built with convict labour in 1829 from the main settlement to Eagle Farm following the river bank after crossing Breakfast Creek. The first narrow footbridge was built over Breakfast Creek in 1840 and was updated in 1848 to hold traffic and again in 1858 because of instability. This road was named Hamilton Road before being changed to Kingsford Smith Drive.

In the early days of the settlement Hamilton became scattered with dairy and pineapple farms. A spring was discovered between the site of the present day Crescent Road and Grays Road and a hotel and brewery built nearby called the Melton Mowbray owned by Mr Bonney. Strangely the brewery failed for lack of a market. The area of Hamilton quickly developed with the advent of trams in 1899.

After the floods of 1890 and 1893, wealthy families built impressive homes on Hamilton's higher ground, with sweeping views of the river.

Pelicans line up at Portside. Photograph by Leo Lapps

Throughout Brisbane's history Hamilton has always been the city's most prestigious suburb, and is generally referred to as one of Brisbane's 'old money' areas. The hill is dominated by grand old Queenslander houses and Victorian style homes. With the addition of the Portside Wharf complex, Hamilton now also features some of Brisbane's most luxurious apartments. This complex was completed just after the turn of the century and is home to the Brisbane Cruise Terminal, and the complex also contains some of Brisbane's best bars and restaurants.

The next stage in Hamilton's evolution is the new Northshore Hamilton development. This will feature a mix of residential and commercial use, as well as large areas of parkland. It will be one of Brisbane's largest urban renewal projects and is on land which was previously part of the Port of Brisbane.

Due to Hamilton's large concentration of Brisbane's grandest homes it is unlikely to lose its standing as the most desirable suburb in the city.

Portside Cruise Terminal

Hamilton Reach Park at Night. Photograph by Australand

Sir Leo Heilsher Bridges (formerly called The Gateway Bridge before the second bridge was erected) taken from the Royal Queensland Golf Club looking up the first fairway. Photograph by Hugh Springer

River View at Hamilton Reach. Photograph by Australand

Sun Princess in port in Hamilton, Brisbane

HAMILTON ISLAND, QUEENSLAND, 1867

Hamilton Island is the largest of the 74 islands that make up the Whitsundays. Like most islands in the Whitsunday group, Hamilton Island was formed as sea levels rose creating numerous drowned mountains that are situated just off the east coast of Queensland, Australia.

As to the origin of the name 'Hamilton', the Port Denison Times of 30 March 1867 reports a cricket match between the crew of Salamander and a Bowen side on 27 March 1867. The surnames of the two sides are given and include a 'Hamilton' on Salamander's team (he scored a total of 3 runs during the match which was won by the ship's team, 69 to 62).

This may have been Sub-Lieutenant Sydney A. R. Hamilton whose name appears in navy lists of 1866- 67 for HMS Curacoa which was on the Australia station at the time. There was some interchange of crew between the two ships as witness Duke D. Yonge of Curacoa who temporarily commanded Salamander before Nares' arrival. Hamilton's name does not appear on navy lists for Salamander but temporary interchanges often were not recorded in the lists. This was the case with Yonge whose time on Salamander was revealed by sources other than the lists.

It is a feature of Nares' survey that the names given originally on his chart and in sailing directions were not all adopted and obviously there were some changes of mind between first and final namings. It is therefore possible that the naming of Hamilton Island, though appearing first on Virago's survey chart may have in fact originated from Salamander. It is significant that Nares gave names of his crew to many islands in the area and as there obviously was a 'Hamilton' among his crew it is a not unreasonable assumption that is where the name originated.

Until just 250 years ago, the magnificence of the Whitsunday Islands and the Great Barrier Reef was known only to a small group of nomadic Aborigines.

At this time the Aborigines of the Ngaro tribe lived off the land and sea here in the Whitsundays whilst sheltering in caves and bark huts on the islands and nearby

Above Right: Whitehaven Beach
Below Right: Heart Reef makes up part of the Great Barrier Reef

Catseye Beach on Hamilton Island

mainland. Their lives were to change when Captain James Cook, who was in the process of charting the east coast of Australia, arrived on HMS Endeavour. They would have been astounded by the size of this vessel as their own mode of water transport was simple dugout canoes.

Although this was some 150 years after the Pilgrims had arrived and settled in America, and only six years before the Declaration of Independence was signed, this particular part of our planet was still unknown to the Western World. It had long been thought that there was a large southern continent in the Pacific, and the King of England, George III, commissioned Cook to make a thorough search for this undiscovered landmass.

Cook and his crew were overwhelmed by the magnificent sight of some 150 tropical islands in close proximity to the coast. Cook called the group the Cumberland Isles, but as time passed those islands adjacent to the Whitsunday passage became more commonly known as 'The Whitsundays'.

As Endeavour continued through the island-studded Whitsunday Passage at a leisurely pace, Cook was taken by the beauty of the region, documenting in his log: 'Everywhere good anchorages, indeed the whole passage is one continued safe harbour.' He also noted the presence of the local Aborigines: 'On one of the islands we discovered with our glasses two men and a woman, and a canoe with an outrigger, which appeared to be larger and of a construction very different from those of bark tied together at the ends, which we had seen upon other parts of the coast.'

It was more than 15 years after the establishment of the convict settlement of Sydney in 1788, before the Whitsundays were visited by Europeans again. This was when Matthew Flinders sailed by while undertaking the incredible task of circumnavigating the entire continent and surveying as much of it as possible. During this circumnavigation, Flinders actually walked on the reefs which he referred to as the 'Extensive Barrier Reefs', and this reference is believed to have contributed to the adoption of the name, the Great Barrier Reef. The coastal region of the Whitsundays was not settled by Europeans until the mid-1800s when farmers looking for potential land moved up from the south. They were mainly timber-getters, graziers and sugarcane farmers, and it wasn't long before they made their way east to the coast where they discovered for themselves the true beauty of the islands. Some were so impressed by the grasslands and forests on the islands that they applied for grazing leases for them.

Tourism began in the 1920s when makeshift huts appeared on some islands and

Qualia – Hamilton Island's luxury resort

along the coast to accommodate local residents and holidaymakers who came from the inland (the 'outback') and the south. The small, idyllic coastal village of Airlie Beach came into existence in 1936, but it was not until the 1970s that the Whitsundays became as strongly synonymous with tourism as they are today. That was the period when the first significant yacht charter companies began to operate out of nearby Shute Harbour.

The real uplift in tourism arrived in the early 1980s with the development of the gateway to the Whitsundays and Great Barrier Reef: Hamilton Island. In the mid-1970s high profile Queensland tourism entrepreneur, Keith Williams, was on a cruise through the Whitsundays aboard his large motor yacht. He noticed an island he hadn't seen

before - it was Hamilton Island, and he realised that it had one of the very few north-facing beaches to be found anywhere on the east coast of Australia. He made some inquiries about the island, and it wasn't long before he and business associate Bryan Byrt had purchased the grazing lease that gave them ownership of the entire two-square mile island. Byrt passed away in 1978, and Williams abandoned plans for establishing a grazing property on the island. Instead he saw the potential for an exciting tourist destination. He built a commercial airport, marina and resort and by the early 1980s Hamilton Island had become Australia's premier tropical island resort destination.

It was when Keith Williams was in the early stages of the development of his resort that noted Australian winemaker Bob Oatley was cruising through the islands aboard a yacht and just happened to sail past Hamilton Island: 'I didn't go ashore, but I could recognise the potential of the island,' Oatley said. 'It was the very early days of the development; they were building the airstrip and the harbour at the time, and there was a lot of activity going on. I remember saying "what a great project that is," never thinking that one day I'd be the owner.' Bob Oatley and his family purchased Hamilton Island in 2003 and, following an exceptional investment and development programme, they now present a world-class destination that promises leisure, lifestyle, adventure and escape in a region of incredible natural beauty.

Hamilton Island is superbly situated to explore the Great Barrier Reef and offers a wide range of activities such as sailing, golf, bushwalking, fishing, tennis and squash.

Hamilton Island is 650 hectares - 5kms from north to south and 3.5kms from east to west, with more than 70% still natural bushland. The island is now a world class tourist destination and was featured in the successful "Best Job in the World" promotion. A number of major films have been on location at Hamilton Island including Muriel's Wedding and Fool's Gold.

Above Left: Aerial View of Hamilton Island
Below Left: Snorkelling on the Great Barrier Reef
All Photographs and bulk of text courtesy of Hamilton Island Enterprises

The Italian Café Scene

Greek Orthodox Church in Hamilton

Typical Early Hamilton Home

HAMILTON, NEWCASTLE, NSW, 1871

Hamilton, Newcastle, New South Wales may be a little different to all the other Hamiltons in that because of the Italian and now Greek influence it is known in some local circles as Am eel Tonne!!

There are possibly as many as 60 restaurants and food outlets along Beaumont Street commercial strip which is perhaps two kilometres long.

Camerons Hill is a spot which was latterly called Scotsmans Hill because it overlooked the then greyhound track and offered free viewing!

The discovery of coal near St Peter's Church in the area known as Cameron's Hill, was the beginnings for the township of Hamilton (originally known as Pittown, Borehole or Happy Flat). A borehole was sunk and a shaft was completed in 1849 and was known as the D Pit, or borehole. Pittown grew up somewhere in the vicinity of today's Beaumont Street to service the needs of the miners and their families.

Hamilton became a municipality on 11 December 1871 and was named in honour of Edward Terrick Hamilton, who was Governor of the board of directors of the Australian Agricultural Company (AA Company), from August 1857 to September 1898. The AA Company was instrumental in the growth of the area, operating the mines and

owning most of the land. The AA Company, formed in the UK, owned the majority of the Hamiltons which have now spread to become Hamilton East, Hamilton South, and Hamilton North. Hamilton South is among the most expensive real estate in Newcastle.

By 1928 there were over 400 retail outlets in Hamilton, having increased from 80 in 1909.

The settling of the Lettesi in Newcastle is an example of the importance of family and regional ties in the building of many Italian communities in New South Wales. This settler group is made up of nearly 150 families from the village of Lettopalena in the Abruzzo region of Italy. Their process of immigration began in the 1920s when a number of Lettesi travelled from the cane fields of Proserpine, Queensland to work the off season at the BHP steel works in Newcastle. During the Second World War the village of Lettopalena suffered major destruction at the hands of Nazi troops and so Proserpine, and then Newcastle became a major focus for a chain migration exodus. In 1947 the Lettesi initially settled in the Islington area but they soon expanded in to the nearby suburbs of Hamilton and Mayfield. This was primarily due to Islington's proximity to the BHP steel works. Before long Hamilton (especially Beaumont Street) was to become a strong community and commercial centre for Newcastle's Italians.

By the late fifties, the local Italian community began patronising the Australian owned Exchange Hotel, located on the corner of Beaumont and Denison Streets. It continues to be a regular meeting place for the Italian men of Hamilton.

On 28th December, 1989 at 10:29am a magnitude 5.6 earthquake shook the city of Newcastle and its surrounds, killing 13 people and hospitalising 162 others. 300,000 people were affected and 1,000 people were made homeless.

Around 50,000 buildings were damaged. Approximately 40,000 of these were homes. 300 buildings were demolished and more than one third of these were homes.

Over 70,000 insurance claims were received. The total insurance pay-out in 1996 dollar terms amounted to A$1.02 billion. The total financial cost of the earthquake is estimated to have amounted to about A$4 billion

Above Left: Kent Tavern – One of the earthquake affected buildings
Below Left: Clock Tower
Photographs by David Brown

EDWARD WILLIAM TERRICK HAMILTON (1809-1898)

Edward William Terrick Hamilton was a British businessman and politician who spent fifteen years as a pastoralist in New South Wales.

Born in Loughton, Essex, he was the son of the Reverend Anthony Hamilton and his wife Charity, née Farquhar. His older brother, Walter Kerr Hamilton, was Bishop of Salisbury from 1854 – 1869.

Hamilton was educated at Eton College and Trinity College, Cambridge. He graduated with a B.A. in 1832 and M.A. in 1835 and was made a fellow of the college in 1834. He was called to the bar at the Inner Temple in 1832.

Hamilton decided not to take up a legal career, instead choosing to take up "pastoralism" or the raising of livestock in New South Wales, with the aim of making a sufficient fortune to return to England and live as a gentleman of leisure. In 1839 he purchased a cattle and sheep station near Cassilis, New South Wales with his cousin, Captain H G Hamilton, RN and friend George Clive. He moved to New South Wales in February 1840 to manage the station, and remained there for 15 years. He was nominated to the New South Wales Legislative Council in 1843. He resigned from the body in 1846, was re-appointed in 1848, serving until 1850. He married Ann Thacker of Berkshire and New South Wales in August 1844. In 1851 he was appointed the first provost of the University of Sydney, resigning in 1854.

In January 1855 Hamilton returned to England, having sold his shares in the livestock stations. He was appointed chairman of the London-based Australian Agricultural Company in 1857, a position he held until his death. He was also appointed chairman of the Bank of Australasia.

At the 1865 general election Hamilton was elected to the Parliament of the United Kingdom as one of two members of parliament for the City of Salisbury. In August 1869 Hamilton resigned his parliamentary seat.

Hamilton continued with his business activities until his death. He maintained his links with New South Wales, and was the colony's representative agent in London for some years. He made his home at Charters, Sunningdale, Berkshire, and was appointed High Sheriff in 1879. He died there in 1898 survived by two sons and six daughters.

Other Hamiltons in Australia

Hamilton River, Western Australia is a tributary of the Collie River in the South West region of Western Australia.

Hamilton River, Queensland is a tributary of the Georgina River. The ruins of the Hamilton Hotel can be seen here.

Hamilton River, South Australia is a small river in the northernmost region of the state of South Australia.

Mount Hamilton is a 1,019 feet mountain peak in Tasmania.

Mount Hamilton is a 958 feet mountain peak near Ararat, Victoria.

Mount Hamilton is the highest point (433m) of Macquarie Island, an Australian sub Antarctic Island under the jurisdiction of Tasmania.

New Zealand

HAMILTON, WAIKATO, 1864

Hamilton, known as Kirikiriroa in Māori, is the centre of New Zealand's fourth largest urban area and Hamilton City is the country's fourth largest territorial authority and the largest inland city. Hamilton is in the Waikato Region of the North Island, approximately 130 kilometres south of Auckland. The city is situated at a major road and rail junction in the centre of the Waikato Basin and lies either side of the Waikato River, New Zealand's longest river which flows for 16 kilometres through the city. Hamilton has a mild climate and moderate year round rainfall which keeps the city and the surrounding area very green.

The earliest recorded settlers in this area were Māori from the Tainui waka who called an area on the west bank of the Waikato River Kirikiriroa, meaning long stretch of gravel, which remains the Māori name for Hamilton today.

The Hamilton area has a history of 700-800 years of Māori occupation and settlement, highlighted by pā sites or fortifications, traditional gardens and agricultural features along the Waikato River. In December 2011 several rua or food storage pits were found near the Waikato River bank, close to the Waikato museum. The main hapu, or subtribes, of Hamilton/Kirikiriroa and the surrounding area are Ngati Wairere, Ngati Haua and Ngati Mahanga.

Local Māori were the target of raids by Ngāpuhi during the Musket Wars (1818-1832), and several pā sites from this period can still be found beside the Waikato River. Missionaries had arrived in the area in the 1830s and before the Waikato Kingitanga wars of 1863-64 they estimated that Kirikiriroa had a population of about 78, while at the same time the government estimated the Waikato area had a Māori population of 3,400. By the time British settlers arrived after 1863, most of these Māori villages had been abandoned as the inhabitants were away fighting with the Kingitanga rebels

Above Right: Aerial View of City
Below Right: The Artspost Building

further west in the battlefields of the upper Waipa river.

In 1863, the New Zealand Settlement Act enabled land to be taken from Māori by the Crown. This resulted in 1.2 million hectares of land being confiscated in the Waikato region, and part of this land provided the basis for European settlement in Hamilton. At the end of the Waikato Campaign in the New Zealand Wars the four regiments of the Waikato Militia were settled as a peace-keeping force across the region.

Formal European settlement was established on 24 August 1864, when Captain William Steele came off the gunboat Rangiriri and established the first redoubt near what is now known as Memorial Park. The town was named by Colonel William Moule after Captain John Fane Charles Hamilton, the popular Scottish commander of HMS Esk, who was killed in the battle of Gate Pā, Tauranga. A military outpost was set up in Hamilton East, which was originally destined to be the main street of Hamilton. Evidence of planning for the centre of the village can be seen in the 'village square' concept of Steele Park and the planting of 'English' trees along Grey Street. The first

Left: The Earth Blanket (Nga Uri o Hinetuparimaunga) at entrance to Hamilton Gardens
Above: Riff Raff Statue

Char Bagh Garden –Hamilton Gardens

The Italian Garden – Hamilton Gardens

Balloons over Waikato at the Lake Domain

mayor of the fledging town was Isaac R. Vialou, an architect of some renown with several other business interests in the area. He held office until February 1878.

At the time of settlement, two other Māori villages shared the area, one being Te Rapa Pā, the other, on the east side of the river, Miropiko Pā, named after a crooked Miro tree growing on a nearby hilltop.

The Borough of Hamilton was established in 1877 with a population of 1,245 and an area of 752 hectares. In December 1945, Hamilton became a city with 20,000 citizens, and today the population has grown to 145,000.

Hamilton is at the centre of one of the richest agricultural and pastoral areas in the world and although initially primarily an agricultural service centre, the city now has a growing and diverse economy. Education and research and development play an important part in Hamilton's economy, as the city is home to approximately 40,000 tertiary students and 1,000 PhD scientists at the University of Waikato and Wintec, and to a number of New Zealand's science research facilities.

Hamilton Central, on the Waikato River, has a sophisticated and vibrant stretch of bars and eateries and the entertainment area is quite lively due to the large student population. Many of the city's venues and attractions are located close to the City Centre. These include the famous Hamilton Gardens which attract large visitor numbers and is the venue for the City's main Arts Festival, and also Founders Theatre and the new Claudelands Events Centre which attract top performers. The famous 'Balloons over Waikato' event is held in April at various venues around the city. There is an increasing amount of public art including a statue of Riff Raff, from The Rocky Horror Show. (Author Richard O'Brien was resident in Hamilton when he wrote the show.) The Earth Blanket at the entrance to Hamilton Gardens is another interesting piece of work. Waikato Stadium (home of the Waikato and Chiefs Rugby teams) and Seddon Park (Cricket) host regional, national and international sporting events and for 5 years Hamilton has hosted a street race leg of the Australian V8 Championship. The Hamilton Lake Domain is another popular attraction. The city continues to grow rapidly.

Photographs Courtesy of Hamilton City Council

Fairfield Bridge at night

CAPTAIN JOHN CHARLES FANE HAMILTON (1822 – 1864)

John Charles Fane Hamilton was born in Scotland in 1822. His grandfather was MP for Oxford, England, his father a Colonel in the army, and an uncle was a Rear-Admiral. John joined the navy in 1835 at the age of 13. He saw service in many parts of the world, including China, where he was involved in fighting on land and in ship's boats. Hamilton was promoted to Lieutenant in March 1844, at the age of 22 and went on to serve in the Americas and the Crimea. He was promoted to the rank of Commander for his bravery at the Seige of Sebastopol. It was there that his crew presented him with the sword that was later given to the City of Hamilton by his descendants.

He was appointed Captain of the Esk, a corvette of 1,169 tons, and was sent to New Zealand to help in the New Zealand Wars.

At the battle of Gate Pa he had under his direct command a detachment of the 43rd Regiment and a party of sailors. In the words of a nineteenth century historian, "The gallant Hamilton sprang upon the embankment, waved his sword in the air, and shouted, 'Follow me, men!' Scarcely had the words passed his lips when a bullet struck him in the head, his sword dropped from his hand, and he fell to rise no more."

He is buried in a cemetery in Tauranga.

HAMILTONS, CENTRAL OTAGO

Hamiltons has an intriguing and continuous history that is still evident today.

It is situated on the western slopes of the Rock and Pillar mountain range and is approximately twenty minutes drive from Ranfurly and ten kilometres from Waipiata. Hamiltons is close to Patearoa and En Hakkore Religious Retreat, which was originally built as a tuberculosis sanitarium in the 1930s.

The area is named after Captain Hamilton, who along with two others drew up and took up Run 204, known as Hamiltons Station. In late 1863, gold was reported and the field initially proved very rich, yielding thousands of ounces of gold. Some 2,000 miners first worked the area, peaking at 4,000 in 1864. Ironically, the surviving township of Patearoa once relied heavily on Hamiltons for shops and services. The town of Hamiltons, which included 25 liquor outlets and 40 stores, did not last long, although a few miners did stay and continue hydraulic sluicing.

Any sign of the town had all but gone by the early 1900s, although sluicing scars can still be seen and the irrigation dam remains. Alongside Hamilton Road, the restored Hamiltons Cemetery rests behind a stone wall. It is a lonely tribute to Hamiltons past and a wonderful example of history, preserved.

The Waipiata Country Hotel continues the legacy of the ancient ice sport of curling with Hamiltons' Curling Club, which was established in 1886. A distinctive slice of Maniototo's past lies at Hamiltons.

Hamiltons Cemetery. Photograph by Steve Kewish Photography

Hamiltons Dam. Photograph by Steve Kewish Photography

Other Hamiltons in New Zealand

Hamilton River The Hamilton River is a river in the Marlborough region of the South Island of New Zealand. It is a tributary of the Wairau River.

Mount Hamilton Mount Hamilton is a 9,833 feet mountain peak near Hokitika, on the west coast of South Island.

Hamilton Peak Hamilton Peak is a mountain of 6,300 feet in the Craigieburn Range of the Southern Alps.

Africa

HAMILTON, BLOEMFONTEIN, SOUTH AFRICA, 1905

During the Boer War in 1901 the Irishman, Major (later Sir) Hamilton Goold-Adams was put in command when the British forces had taken the Boer republic of the Orange Free State and besieged its capital, Bloemfontein. Over the subsequent period, 1905 -10, Goold –Adams served as Lieutenant-Governor of the Orange River Colony (now Free State). During this time he earned the respect and affection of Boer and British alike.

Thus, in 1905, a railway siding on the new line to Kimberley was named after him, as was the park at the western foot of Naval Hill which opened in 1907. Interestingly his first name, Hamilton, was chosen, which says something.

The suburb of Hamilton now lies south of the city centre, a long triangular piece of land with the acute angle on Hamilton commuter station, and its hypotenuse stretching some 4 kilometres southward abutting Church Street, historically the main access route to Bloemfontein. It is a light industrial area, fitted probably strategically as a buffer, between the black townships of Batho and Bochabela on the east and the Boer War museum, Women's Memorial and Memoriam cemetery and the residential suburbs on the west.

Hamilton is flat like most light industrial areas, but it is has many trees. Judging by the design of the buildings it has been developed from about the 1930s until recently. The street snaking its way through the two black suburbs is called Hamilton Rd while Goold-Adams Street is a minor road among railway housing east of the Bloemfontein station.

Text and Photographs - Professor Wally Peters

Typical view of food store and adjacent financial outlet.

Tree lined street with windmill and silos

Hamilton Station

SIR HAMILTON GOOLD-ADAMS (1858 -1920)

Born in 1858 in the town of Jamesbrook in County Cork, Ireland, Goold-Adams was a cadet on the training ship HMS Conway until he decided to join the British Army. He was commissioned in the Royal Scots Regiment, serving principally in southern Africa, where he achieved the rank of Captain in 1885 and Major in 1895. During the Second Boer War he served first as Resident Commissioner in Bechuanaland and afterwards as Commander of the Town Guard during the latter half of the Siege of Mafeking, where he was twice 'Mentioned in Despatches.'

He was made Deputy Commissioner and later Lieutenant-Governor of the Orange River Colony under Governor Alfred Milner, 1st Viscount Milner, from 1901 to 1907. He was made CMG in 1902 and GCMG in 1907.

He returned to England in 1911 where he married a Canadian named Elsie Riordon on 4 July. Later that year he was appointed British High Commissioner to Cyprus. In 1914 he was made Governor of Queensland, arriving in Brisbane just before the election of Queensland's first majority Labour Government, under Premier T. J. Ryan. He occasionally disapproved of Labour's policies and appointments to the Legislative Council of Queensland.

During his return to England on his retirement, Goold-Adams contracted pleurisy on board ship, and died in Cape Town, South Africa in 1920.

One of the 'tents' in the camp.

Dining overlooking the bush

HAMILTONS TENTED CAMP, 2002

In 2000 South African National Parks decided to develop various private concession areas within the 2 million hectare Kruger National Park. As one of the largest game reserves on earth the "Kruger" was established over 100 years ago. One of the true conservation tracts left in South Africa the bids for concessions were huge.

By establishing these private concessions of land, which were mainly peripheral in the Park, SANParks would allow independent five star hoteliers to develop high end lodges within the boundaries of a national park. It was a first, and highly contested initially.

A bid for the 10,000 hectare Mluwati Concession was successful and building on Hamiltons Tented Camp commenced in early 2002. The location chosen was unique in that it had an existing weir which would ensure almost permanent water in front of the camp. The benefits of this were obviously water being visually aesthetically

pleasing and the fact that such water would attract vast numbers of animals to drink.

Choosing a name for the camp was easy – the nearby Stevenson-Hamilton museum and library (at Skukuza) was a source of discovering the history behind the Kruger. James Stevenson-Hamilton was the first warden of the Sabie Game Reserve, forerunner of the Kruger National Park, from 1902. Literally translated it means 'he who sweeps clean' and refers to Stevenson-Hamilton's efforts to control poaching in the early days.

Reminiscent of a bygone era, Hamiltons Tented Camp dishes up lavish doses of romance, exploration and intrigue. Creating the feel of a lavish tent, each canvas cocoon offers opulent luxury complete with antique mahogany travel chests, Persian rugs and soft white canvas.

Hamiltons Tented Camp reflects a safari adventure of the early twentieth century,

Luxurious Tented Lounge

where grace and style were the epitome of luxurious living. Six magnificent canvas tents complete with teak floorboards, mosquito nets, slipper baths, outdoor showers and a superb view of the seasonal river are linked to the main lodge area by raised timber walkways amongst ancient Jackalberry trees. Uncompromising elegance and breath-taking beauty identifies Hamiltons Tented Camp.

Sip sun downers on the deck and gaze over the river - you never know what you might see. At Hamiltons Tented Camp, we delight in creating delicious feasts using locally grown produce, coupled with excellent wines, in surprise settings. Imagine dining beneath the starlit skies and the distant chorus of nocturnal creatures.

Early morning and afternoon/evening open vehicle safaris take our guests into some of the richest game viewing areas in Kruger. Rewarding moments tracking various members of the animal kingdom in order to record the sighting on film are the stories our guests take home with them. Bird watching around the camp is phenomenal with many rare species being spotted regularly by enthusiasts!

Photographs and text courtesy of Hamiltons Tented Camp

Water Buffalo at waterhole near the camp

COLONEL JAMES STEVENSON – HAMILTON (1876 – 1957)

James Stevenson-Hamilton was born the eldest of nine children in Scotland on the 2nd of October 1876. Being first born he was the legal heir to their family title and home at Fairholm, near Larkham in Scotland. He was educated at Rugby and Sandhurst and opted for a career in the military.

He saw active service with the Inniskillings in Natal in 1888. In 1898 he had joined the Cape-to-Cairo expedition under the leadership of Major A St H Gibbons. Once they had steamed up the Zambesi in flat bottomed launches and fought their way well beyond the Kariba Gorge they had to abandon their boats and explore Barotseland on foot. Stevenson-Hamilton then trekked across Northern Rhodesia to the Kafue. After the expedition he returned to the military and fought in the Second-Anglo-Boer War receiving the Queen's medal and the King's medal for his service.

In 1902 Sir Godfrey Lagden appointed James Stevenson-Hamilton as the warden of the Sabie Game reserve. As a bachelor, a man of means and a professional soldier Lagden deemed him fit for the job, even though the post was viewed as unusual and unheard of. Stevenson-Hamilton signed a two year contract as warden, found a map of the area and set off with a wagon, oxen, provisions and ammunition for an uncharted and malaria filled land described to him as the "white man's grave" . Game-ranging was still a new term and this allowed Stevenson-Hamilton to have free reign over the Sabie Game reserve, his only order from Lagden being "to make himself generally disagreeable" and try and put an end to poaching.

In 1902 he reached Nelspruit. His first order of business was to announce that no shooting was to be allowed and that if he and his servant could live on tinned meat, so could the European settlers and indigenous people who were inclined to shoot an impala whenever they felt the need . He believed that if there was no shooting, if animals were left to live in the veld as they had lived before man came on the scene, they would lose their fear of human beings and flock to an area that had once been described as "red with impala". He then moved his headquarters from Crocodile Bridge to Sabie Bridge and appointed two rangers, the most famous of them Harry Wolhuter, and together they trained native rangers. Poachers soon realised that he was serious about the "no shooting" rule and many were caught including, on one occasion, a party of senior policemen who were caught killing a giraffe and wildebeest and were convicted and fined for their crimes. He trained his rangers, thinned out the lions and the wild dogs, declared war on the poachers and patrolled the whole area. He also became the magistrate, customs collector and border guard as well as watcher of the railway line to the south of the reserve. After this his focus went back to Johannesburg and Pretoria where he started to convince companies in the vicinity to lend him land, eventually giving him a huge block in a remote corner of Transvaal. By doing this he created the space that is known today as the Kruger National Park, extending the reserve from the original 1,200 square miles to 14,000 square miles. Game could therefore roam freely from the Crocodile to the Limpopo River.

In 1904 he was summoned back to war and Stevenson-Hamilton was destined to become the commander of his regiment, the 6th Inniskilling Dragoons. Unable to resign, he asked for extended leave instead - he had grown too fond of Africa. England lost a soldier and South Africa gained a warden.

In the following 20 years Stevenson-Hamilton created history through his ability to protect and regulate the park. In 1912 he first presented his idea for the nationalization of the park to the then Minister of Foreign Affairs, Jan Smuts. The idea was to transform the reserve into a National Park, but to do this he needed the support of the public, which meant allowing visitors into the Park. Unfortunately the war temporarily halted these events. In 1926 Piet Grobler established the National Parks Bill in parliament as encouraged by Stevenson-Hamilton and presented the park as a realization of the dreams of Paul Kruger and therefore renamed the Sabie Game Reserve the Kruger National Park of South Africa. In 1927, the Park was opened to the public who were charged a £1 entry fee.

Stevenson-Hamilton served the game reserve for 44 years, from 1902 to 1946, and after his retirement settled down in White River. At the age of 63 he married Hilda Cholmondeley, and they had three children. He died in 1957 at the age of ninety.

HAMILTON, SIERRA LEONE

Hamilton is the English name for the village otherwise known as Kangbe, meaning "the original." It is located around the Freetown Peninsula. It is an original Creole Village that has a fine beach, poultry farms, large back yards, and houses with wide verandas. The people are often called "Kangbe Creole," meaning Original Creoles, although some think Kangbe Creoles are mixed Creoles with some Loko addition.

Above Right: Hamilton Beach Restaurant! Photograph by David Vaucher
Below Right: Beach House of one of the wealthy few!

Other Hamiltons in Africa

HAMILTON FALLS, MALAWI

Hamilton Falls (also known as Kapachira Falls), west of Blantyre have recently been visually ruined by the creation of a power station. They are still quite dramatic though, as you can see below.

Photograph by Jim Laybourne

HAMILTONBERGE, NAMIBIA

Hamiltonberge is a 1,033 feet mountain peak, and the area around it near Walvis Bay, Erongo, Namibia.

HAMILTON MOUNTAIN, SIERRA LEONE

Hamilton Mountain is a 1,213 feet mountain peak near Hastings, Western Area, Sierra Leone.

HAMILTON, ZIMBABWE

Hamilton is a suburb of Glendale, just south of Bindura.

Other Hamiltons

HAMILTONY, CZECH REPUBLIC, 1764

The settlement is part of Hamilton City, Vyškov. It has belonged to the estate Vyškov Terriers since 1764. The original name was Hamiltonky until 1784.

The name of the village derives from the Bishop of Olomouc and Count Maximilian of Hamilton for whom the village was founded.

The village lies in a narrow valley of the Great Hana, north of Vyškov. Within the village are the castle ruins, (located across from the chapel on a high mound, Strachotínka) and the pseudo chapel of Cyril and Methodius from 1871, popularly called Strachotínka (according to the old Czech version of the name Methodius Strachota). It is where people were allegedly baptized by the missionaries Cyril and Methodius.

Chapel Strachotinka. Photograph by Zbynek.Havacek

MAXIMILIAN REICHSGRAF VON HAMILTON, BISHOP OF OLOMOUC (1714 – 1776)

Furstbischof Maximilian Reichsgraf von Hamilton was a Prince-Bishop of Olomouc, then in the Holy Roman Empire, now in the present day Czech Republic.

Hamilton's family originally came from Scotland, where his great-great grandfather was James Hamilton, 1st Earl of Abercorn. Hamilton's grandfather was on the council of the Elector of Bavaria, was the Landvogt to the Margrave of Burgau, and also a chamberlain to the Holy Roman Emperor. He was given, in 1698, the imperial title of Count of Neuburg. Hamilton's parents were Julius Francis Hamilton, Reichsgraf von Neuburg, and Maria Ernestina von Stahrenberg.

Hamilton was born in Munich, educated at Ettal Abbey, and graduated in 1738 from the Sapienza in Rome. After his ordination in 1738 he became a pastoral worker and in 1747 Canon of Olomouc, in 1751 rector of St. Anne's Chapel at the Cathedral of Olomouc and in 1758 was appointed Vicar General. After the death of Prince-Bishop Leopold Friedrich von Egkh and Hungersbach, he was elected as his successor by the cathedral chapter of Olomouc. He died in Kroměříž.

HAMILTON CANAL, COLOMBO, SRI LANKA, 1801

During the 15th century, Negambo lagoon served as the main seaport for Colombo. The Sinhalese king of the time began to cut a canal and this work was continued by the Dutch settlers to link the Kelani River with the seaport of Negambo.

The Dutch, during their time in Ceylon improved the canal system of the area. Gavin Hamilton, British Agent of Revenue and Commerce, in 1801 started a new canal to the east of the earlier cut canal by the Sinhalese king and the Dutch. (Unfortunately after his death, in 1804, he was found to have embezzled nearly 20,000 pounds. This very large sum was recovered from his estate.)

The Hamilton Canal was named after him and it was meant to link the Dutch canal by a series of parallel canals designed to drain the Muturajawela. However what happened was the opposite as the high tide brought salinity not only from Negambo lagoon but also the Kelani River. To cash in on this, a few entrepreneurs started making salt and the government had to prosecute villages who started the salt business. Hamilton Canal then earned the epithet of "Hamilton's Folly" and the local name Moda Ela or Foolish Canal. The canal is maintained periodically and rock-fill work is done where banks are eroded. Hotels in the vicinity are interested in developing the canals for water sports such as rowing, boating, sailing, water-skiing and paddle boating.

Related leisure time activities are also planned which would mean the construction of boat-houses, restaurants on land and on the water, cafes and gardens or parks thus linking the waterways with the adjoining land. The SLLRDC intends joining the Hamilton Canal with the Colombo network to develop the tourist industry as well as for transport of public and produce.

Photographs by Ruwan Pinnawela

PORT HAMILTON, SOUTH KOREA, 1845

Port Hamilton or Komundo, officially Geomun-do in Korean, is a small group of islands in the Jeju Strait off the southern coast of the Korean Peninsula. There are three principal islands, the two larger ones, Sodo to the west and Sunhodo to the east forming a harbour with the smaller island in the centre. On this central island, Observatory Island (or Go-do), there was a British naval base from 1885 to 1887. Today, the islands form a part of Samsan District, Yeosu City, South Jeolla Province, with the Samsan District offices located on Observation Island. The islands are also part of the Dadohae Haesang National Park.

Port Hamilton was surveyed in 1845 by British naval officer Sir Edward Belcher in HMS Samarang and was named after the then Secretary of the Admiralty, Captain W. A. Baillie-Hamilton. The spacious harbour was also noted for its strategic importance by others, such as Russian Vice-Admiral Yevfimy Putyatin, who visited the islands several times and obtained permission from locals in 1857 to establish a coal depot, though due to delays in the delivery of the coal the plan was abandoned.

In 1884 the United States Secretary of the Navy urged the establishment of a naval station at Port Hamilton, and although it appears that such facilities were offered by the Korean government, nothing was done.

In April 1885, Port Hamilton was occupied by three ships of the British Royal Navy, on orders from the Admiralty, in what is known as the Port Hamilton Incident. This was to forestall Russian advances in the face of the Panjdeh Incident in Afghanistan. Port Hamilton served as a counterbalance to the Russian naval base at Vladivostok. By occupying Port Hamilton, the British could prevent Russian advances in East Asia, and block Russian naval activity in the Korea Strait. The British built a few buildings and defensive works and introduced pheasants to the islands. Permission was obtained from China for a cable to be landed at Saddle Island (at the mouth of the Yangtze River). From there, the cable could be connected to the main telegraphic network at Shanghai, thus enabling telegraph communication with Port Hamilton.

After the Russian threat had diminished the British demolished the base and left on 27 February 1887, though they continued to frequent the islands. The visits were less frequent after 1910, when the Japanese Empire annexed Korea.

Until the end of World War II, a Japanese graveyard stood in Port Hamilton. When Japanese claims to the islands were specifically renounced in the Treaty of San Francisco, the Japanese graves were removed, but a British graveyard remains up to this day and has become a tourist attraction. Ten British sailors and marines are buried on the islands including two sailors from HMS Albatross, who were killed in March 1886 when their gun exploded, and a young sailor, Alex Wood, from HMS Albion, who died in 1903.

Photographs by Jay Hyuck Shin

ADMIRAL WILLIAM ALEXANDER BAILLIE-HAMILTON (1803-1881)

Admiral William Alexander Baillie-Hamilton was a British naval commander.

A member of the Baillie-Hamilton family headed by the Earl of Haddington, he was the son of the Venerable Charles Baillie, Archdeacon of Cleveland and his wife Lady Charlotte Home, daughter of Alexander Home, 9th Earl of Home. His brothers also gained distinction. Sir George Baillie was Ambassador to Tuscany; Charles Baillie-Hamilton was a politician; Ker Baillie-Hamilton was Governor of the Leeward Islands; and Cospatrick Baillie-Hamilton was also an Admiral in the Royal Navy. Baillie-Hamilton served on the Arctic Council when it was searching for Sir John Franklin's ill-fated expedition to find the North West passage. He married Harriet Hamilton, daughter of James Hamilton, Viscount Hamilton, in 1836. They had two daughters and four sons.

He became Second Secretary to the Admiralty in 28 April 1845.

His son, also William, played football for Scotland in the first of the England v Scotland representative matches and was later a senior civil servant. Another son, Charles also played for Scotland in the same match.

MOUNT HAMILTON, ANTARCTICA, 1903

Mount Hamilton stands at the eastern edge of Kent Plateau, 7 miles south of Mount Tuatara. Discovered by the Discovery Expedition it was named for Admiral Sir Richard Vesey Hamilton, who served on Arctic voyages (1850–54) and was a member of the Ship Committee for this expedition.

ADMIRAL SIR RICHARD VESEY HAMILTON (1829 – 1912)

Richard Vesey Hamilton was born in May, 1829 – his father was the Rector of Little Chart in Kent.

Educated at the Royal Naval School in Camberwell, Hamilton joined the Royal Navy in 1843.

In 1852 he served as a lieutenant on HMS Resolute where he was involved in a search for Sir John Franklin's ill-fated expedition to find the North West passage. In 1856 he joined HMS Haughty and took part in the Battle of Fatshan Creek during the Second Opium War. Between 1862 and 1873 he commanded successively Vesuvius, Sphinx and Achilles.

In 1875 Hamilton was made Captain-Superintendent of Pembroke Dock and in 1878 he was appointed Director of Naval Ordnance at the Admiralty. In 1880 he was given a command off the coast of Ireland. He was appointed Commander-in-Chief, China Station in 1885, Second Naval Lord in 1888 and First Naval Lord in 1889. He retired in 1891.

In retirement Hamilton wrote a manual entitled Naval Administration. He died in Chalfont St Peter in Buckinghamshire in 1912.

Other Assorted Hamiltons

A cottage in Hamiltonganj. Photograph by Bimal Krishna Goswami

Sunset over the Basra River near Hamiltonganj.
Photograph by ashdatta@gmail.com

HAMILTONHILL, GLASGOW, SCOTLAND

Hamiltonhill is a working class district situated between Possilpark and Port Dundas in the Scottish city of Glasgow. It is situated north of the River Clyde, next to the Forth and Clyde Canal.

There is a concentration of Chinese people in the area, and as a consequence the area has lots of good Chinese restaurants and stores stocking Chinese made goods.

HAMILTONGANJ, INDIA

Hamiltonganj is situated in the Jalpaiguri district of West Bengal only about 20 miles from the Bhutan border.

AND THEN WE FINISH BY GOING OUT OF THE WORLD

ASTEROID 492 HAMILTONIA, 1899

This asteroid was discovered by astronomers at the Lick Observatory on Mount Hamilton, California! (see page 103)

Acknowledgements

A number of people have been attributed for their photographs or text in the body of the book but there are a large number of other people to thank.

Text and Photograph Gathering:

Scotland

- Stephen Balfour

United States of America

- Norma Berry, Nicole Haake, Mike Hicks, Vince Mitchell,

  Jimmy Sample

Canada

- Tim Hockin

Australia

- Zara Gerven, Kelsey Hodges, John Leddy, Stacey Triffett, Alastair Wilson

New Zealand

- Jeff Neems

Africa

- Kate Davidson

Sri Lanka

- Mely Dharmasena

Book Production

Jean Brooker and Diane Yates

- For their proofreading.

Lisa Ryan

- For the Book's Design.

Bill Wiles, and all at Print House

- For their help in pre-production.

Gordon Chesterman

- For his practical help and encouragement.

Website www.hamiltonsoftheworld.com

Lawrence Van der Helm